R.A.T.E.S.

PRINCIPLES FOR SUCCESSFUL

NONPROFIT AND HUMAN SERVICES

Response-ability, Account-ability, Technical-ability, Evaluation-ability, Sustain-ability

Dr. Margaret Jamal

CONTENTS

PREFACE

The most important resources in human service delivery will always be the human resources. Human service workers need to be empowered and equipped to help eliminate problems for clients. They also need to make a decent living that meets their financial obligations while they work to eliminate the problem.

Many Non-profit and Human Service organizations in underserved communities that have experience with receiving grants or business loans seldom receive adequate training to efficiently manage their projects. In the case of government funds, too many organizations tend to receive just enough money to get in trouble. An organization may propose a project that requests $100,000 and receive $75,000. This $75,000 grant may accompany a contract that binds them to do the same thing that the $100,000 was supposed to accomplish. Many organizations are so delighted to have received *some* money that they do everything in their power to try to meet the proposed grant objectives. However in order to comply with the projected *numerical* outcomes they often sacrifice the *quality* of service.

The leaders of newer organizations are often too afraid to speak about how difficult it was for them to offer the appropriate services for fear of not receiving future funding. As a program consultant, I witnessed this unfortunate dilemma far too often. In one such experience, I attended a meeting held by a donor Foundation that offers funds to a grossly underserved community. The grant-making Director of the foundation informed a grantee Executive Director that if he did not do what they told him to do that he could forget about *ever* receiving any funds from them again. The foundation had initially encouraged this organization to move forward while commending their commitment to end homelessness. However the donor foundation was more interested in developing real estate than in ending homelessness.

A primary concern was that the foundation had already given money for the struggling organization to complete a building project. However the dollar amount that was offered was not enough to finish the project, so the Executive Director frantically sought other funding options to get the project completed. He was steered to an organization that was supposed to make no-interest loans to grass roots organizations and also to a state funding program. The state funding program manager sent the hopeful Executive Director through all sorts of hoops assuring him that when each "I" was dotted and every "T" was properly crossed that he would qualify for the grant dollars.

This motivated Executive Director fervently tried to apply for other funds as well. Unfortunately, he did not have enough time to get all of the paper work done to solicit more funds because he worked a full time job. He worked a full time job because the donors have a general practice of frowning upon paying for executive directors' support. Although he worked overtime to get the money that was supposed to come from the state, he did not get it. As time went on, the building was vandalized and had more damage done to it.

The money that was not enough in the first place was now chipping away for maintenance. To add to the problems, the courts demanded that the building be secured by a vendor rather than by the organization. This court ordered debt was incurred by the organization-without additional help from any donors. All the while the initial Foundation was against giving *any more* money to the project. Then the Foundation made an offer to pay for a project director, but would not support the executive director that had established the relationships with the city and potential donors.

Although the adequate amount of money was not given by the parties that was asked, the Executive Director still sought to provide low income housing because he remained committed to the problem of homelessness. However the partnership of non-profit to donor was *not* mutually beneficial because the donor was not as committed to ending homelessness.

The problem of homelessness or any other societal problem is not going to be solved simply by building houses. The presence of so many abandoned buildings and unoccupied houses is evidence of this. Simple solutions to societal issues such as homelessness or even unemployment fall short of what is needed to truly change what is wrong. I found that many grassroots organizations understand the complex needs of their communities, but were seldom afforded adequate resources to maintain successful programs.

For organizations to make a significant impact, they must develop methods for maximizing their resources while enhancing service delivery according to identified needs. The grassroots organizations, that really have a stake in community improvement often find it difficult to take advantage of funds that may be available. The R.A.T.E.S. Principles were initially developed in response to my attempts to teach well meaning organizations how to develop an effective federal grant proposal in order to qualify for available funds. After my first grant writing courses were developed, some reoccurring questions from my students prompted me to set up a workshop that would lay a foundation that would prepare them to truly benefit from a grant writing session.

I found that many of my students had organizational questions that should have been addressed *prior* to attending a grant proposal writing class. For example, most of those who attended had questions about what *program activities* they should include in the proposal. They were not asking about the programs that already existed, but wanted help with *structuring* their programs. I also realized that most of my students had not first established their own organizational identities.

R.A.T.E.S. Principles offer a universal platform of developmental and operational standards for non-profit human services. This platform provides a consistent point of reference in order to accommodate organizational as well as leadership development. R.A.T.E.S is an acronym for five essential areas of development which are Response-ability, Account-ability, Technical-ability, Evaluation-ability and Sustain-ability. Each of these five categories may include any number of sub categories that can offer a continuum of learning and development. Those organizations that function according to the R.A.T.E.S. Principles will establish and be able to demonstrate a firm foundation upon which to build and continue their efforts towards making the world better for us all.

Typically by the time you decide that you want to start a non-profit project, you have determined that something wrong in society is not being properly addressed. You may have also decided that you want to get paid for working to make a difference. Or you may have a different reason for considering how to become a non-profit. No matter what your motivation may be, you will still need to understand some basic principles for establishing and maintaining your non-profit organization.

My own experience in the non-profit arena taught me that certain standard practices are essential in establishing a viable and lasting initiative to effect change. I developed the R.A.T.E.S. Principles to offer a solid platform of universal organizational practices that could easily lend itself to teaching others. I have observed these standards to be consistent in successful programs.

Also, the R.A.T.E.S. Principles encompass an assembling of these organizational standards in order to springboard a fundamental understanding and method of learning and instruction. R.A.T.E.S. is intended to first satisfy the burden of answering the question, "where do I start?" In the course of deciding upon technical assistance, capacity building or organizational development, the non-profit arena has remained without a universally adaptable, foundational starting point. I believe that the R.A.T.E.S. Principles address this need.

WHAT EXACTLY IS R.A.T.E.S.?

R..A.T.E.S is an acronym for five essential areas of development which are Response-ability, Account-ability, Technical-ability, Evaluation-ability and Sustain-ability. Each of these five categories may include any number of sub categories that can offer a continuum of learning and development.

The five R.A.T.E.S. categories are briefly defined as follows:

Response-ability is having and demonstrating the ability to give a favorable response to problems and needs. The critical needs that must be considered are those of the leadership, client, staff, partners, donors and the organization as a whole.

Account-ability is having and demonstrating the ability to account for program and fiscal activities along with associated resources.

Technical-ability is having and demonstrating the ability to apply technology in order to maximize productivity. It also includes having the ability to engage the technical communication, practices and policies that govern an area of interest.

Evaluation-ability is having and demonstrating the ability to engage an independent and unbiased evaluator who will assess the strengths and challenges of an organization and related projects. The results of the evaluations will help develop strategies for ongoing improvements. The techniques for planning an evaluation will also help strengthen program structure and efficiency.

Sustain-ability is having and demonstrating the ability to continue providing support and development for an organization through diverse and effective resource and revenue development activities.

The better organizational leaders are with applying the R.A.T.E.S. Principles the better they will operate their organizations. These areas also make practitioners better able to grasp the concepts that make up a grant proposal. Understanding and applying the concepts for grant proposal development help to set and maintain organizational structure.

It became apparent to me that the majority of my Grant Writing Workshop attendees tended to sign up for grant writing classes after finding out about an opportunity to obtain grant funds. However, they were generally unsure about what they needed to write in the proposal in order to obtain the funds. Because of the questions, I realized that they did not understand that their grant proposal was supposed to *reflect their ability* and experience with solving the problems that the funds were offered to address. They also needed to understand how they were going to have to operate as a non-profit organization in order to *continue* to receive adequate resources to sustain their programs.

Considering the lack of readily available resources to help start-up non-profit organizations at that time, I appreciated the questions as legitimate and necessary to address. Some of the most common questions from students included: Who should I hire? How much should people get paid? What services can I offer? How can I get a building? How much money should I ask for? However my experience taught me that they needed more than just an answer to these questions. They needed to know how to think in order to develop the answers to those questions for themselves.

I have observed that there is a clear advantage in the ability to plan effective program strategies with those who demonstrate their commitment to practicing the R.A.T.E.S. Principles. Additionally, grant proposal strategies were more apparently understood by those who were applying R.A.T.E.S. Principles than by those who were unfamiliar with R.A.T.E.S. concepts. The material contained in this learning workbook is intended to equip readers, students and committed change makers with information and strategic thinking that will result in their developing, providing and maintaining successful non-profit and human services.

Response-ability is having and demonstrating the ability to give a favorable response to problems and needs. A favorable response is one that causes the receiver to agree that a need has been met and is no longer problematic.

Non-profits need to first learn a process for establishing their area of commitment and expertise regarding an identified problem. Identifying a specific problem helps them to build upon an effort with which they are more likely to be successful. It also allows them to have consistency and continuity with planning and providing favorable responses to needs that emerge from the established problems. This process of identifying problems and needs develop useful information for producing *problem* and *needs* statements. Participants will first learn a technique to focus upon identifying a specific problem to eliminate. Then the *needs statements* will be developed as they relate to projected solutions for the stated problems. This process is designed to encourage and demonstrate commitment to make a measurable improvement based upon a specific and targeted area of interest. In planning responses to needs, participants will also learn how to plan for adequate resources.

There is a hierarchy of needs that should be addressed when considering *Response-ability*. The first need is that of the visionary and founder who also tends to be the primary *service provider*. Service providers do something to improve a situation. They are the people who feel compelled to make a difference regarding problems or injustice that they have decided have continued long enough. However, this visionary rarely assesses the extent of needs for herself or himself. They are much more concerned with servicing the needs of those that they believe are suffering.

Unfortunately this lack of attention to their own needs too often leads to their ultimate retreat from the effort altogether. More frequently than not, their frustration is due to a significant lack of adequate resources. They frequently misdiagnose their needs to only be for money, when they actually have other *developmental* needs that contribute to their ability to sustain.

For example service providers need to know *what problem*(s) they are committed to solve as well as *who* they are committed to help. They also need to believe that *they* are the ones who *can* and *must* make a difference. Without these three elements in place there is no real foundation for moving forward.

When you are faced with having a number of problems that concern you, you need to have a method of determining which problem you should address *first*. This does not mean that you cannot address other problems later, but you need a single one to develop in order to have a foundation strong enough to sustain the challenges that will come from supporters and others.

When you decide to start a nonprofit organization you need to plan for giving a favorable response to needs expressed by those that you want to help. You have to plan the responses to what will generally be expected of you. As the one taking responsibility for the success of your non-profit organization you are a *charitable* or *social entrepreneur*.

An entrepreneur takes on the responsibility for launching a business venture. This person realizes that even if everyone else decides to quit, s/he must remain to organize and operate the business. The entrepreneur assumes the risks for the expenses and efforts needed to promote and sustain a business venture. A *social entrepreneur* finds solutions *for* social problems.

Charitable or social entrepreneurs are unique in that their businesses exist to reduce or eliminate human suffering for others. A charitable entrepreneur needs to know that the effort to eliminate human suffering requires a well planned and full time effort. The effort cannot be satisfied by occasional volunteers, but by dedicated staff and consistent support. The support given to those who are suffering generally includes offering a service. Therefore most social or charitable entrepreneurs are also considered to be *service providers*. Social service providers find ways to offer help for others that will somehow improve our society.

In order to be most effective it is important for service providers to have the goal to *eliminate* a specific problem. Trying to eliminate a problem may appear to be a huge task, but we have successes to model in those who sought to rid the world of pain and suffering.

For example the program called Mothers Against Drunk Driving has a mission to completely eliminate drunk driving in the United States. According to a 2006 press release, The organizer and founding president of Mothers Against Drunk Driving also called (MADD) is Candy Lightner whose 13 year old daughter was killed by a drunk driver. Candy Lightner stated the following, "I promised myself on the day of Cari's death that I would fight to make this needless homicide count for something positive in the years ahead,"

The pain and suffering that drunk driving caused Ms. Lightner was the death of her daughter. In eliminating drunk driving, she would also eliminate the suffering and destruction that vehicular homicide causes. One of the challenges that many social entrepreneurs have is that they are not committed to eliminating one specific problem. This can cause them to lose focus and stray from their purpose. This confusion will affect all of the support and resources. Each project must be planned according to the problem that is being eliminated. The need for resources increases with every problem. Therefore, if there are multiple problems that are being addressed at one time, the director has to find more money and resources in order to eliminate each one.

In the example of MADD, Ms. Lightener was compelled to address an issue that challenged her original mission to *eliminate drunk driving*. By 1985, many MADD leaders were calling for the criminalization of all driving after drinking *any* amount of alcoholic beverage. Ms. Lightner did not agree with this ideology. She maintained that police ought to be concentrating their resources on arresting *drunk drivers* rather than on those drivers who happen to have been drinking.

Ms. Lightner stated that MADD "has become far more neo-prohibitionist than I had ever wanted or envisioned … I didn't start MADD to deal with alcohol. I started MADD to deal with the issue of drunk driving"

It is up to the original visionary to keep the focus of the mission. When an organization expands, (such as with MADD) it may attract other people who do not have the same desire to eliminate the same problem. Other people who have not had the same experience may reason that the mission should be altered. It is easier to become side tracked when an organization has more than one problem that is being addressed. However with the focus on a single problem, it is easier to recognize if the original mission is being pushed aside for other interests.

Newly formed grass roots organizations are often started by wonderful visionaries who are passionate about meeting the needs that they have observed and felt. These visionaries soon find that they also want to address a growing number of *related* problems. For example one such visionary (we will call her Mother Snow) wanted to provide a "safe haven" for the children of parents that have been incarcerated and are often wandering the streets searching for love and attention.

Mother Snow, once shared how as a young single mother, she had to work to support her children. This caused them to be alone with nothing constructive to do. Some of her children found themselves in tragic situations that she attributed to a lack of supervision. Mother Snow did not know what she could have done differently, but felt that if her children could have just had a caring responsible home to stay in until she returned from work, life would have been better for them. She later wanted to be for other parents what she wished someone would have been for her.

While Mother Snow was not the child in the streets, she suffered because of her own children being alone and unsupervised. Mother Snow was not trying to start a daycare or anything complicated. She just knew that there were predators looking for unsupervised children to corrupt. She knew that some of her own children had fallen victim to that element and felt the need to turn her pain into a passion for helping others.

Mother Snow started an informal project that the community called, "Safe Haven for Youth." When the parents did not know what to do with their children, they sent them to Mother Snow's Safe Haven. While there, Mother Snow would supervise the youth, encourage them to complete their homework assignments and even play games with them.

One day a young girl in Mother Snow's Safe Haven asked Mother Snow about how to pronounce a word in her reading book. Mother Snow sat down to help the child struggle through her reading assignment. Mother Snow soon realized that many of her children were not doing well in school and needed help with basic reading and writing skills.

While trying to provide tutoring for these children, Mother Snow also found that these children were not eating properly and needed nutritional meals in order to function.

After beginning a feeding program, Mother Snow was informed by some of the children that other people in the community and even people living with them were taking their the snacks from them.

Upon further inquiries, Mother Snow uncovered that many of her children were living in houses that were overrun with illegal and immoral activities. She also learned that (in some cases) visitors and family members were taking advantage of some of these children and abusing them.

Mother Snow tried to address every new problem that would arise until she finally found these needs to be overwhelming. Her own health began to suffer under the increasing stress of trying to protect and care for the children alone. Soon, Mother Snow's Safe Haven was closed to all of the children who were once comforted and sheltered from the streets. Mother Snow was broken hearted knowing that there was no one else who would take up the cause with the love and passion that she had.

Mother Snow felt that she let the children down because she was no longer able to supply the needs for the children. However, her original vision was simply to provide a "safe haven" that would allow these children to get off the streets. Mother Snow could have stayed with her original vision and then sought help from others who already had visions of providing tutoring, nutritional meals and child advocacy. It is important to understand that the original vision can become greatly compromised if other perceived needs begin to use up valuable resources.

In Mother Snow's case (and many others like her), her most valuable resource, which was the human resource, was over taxed to the point of burn out. When there is no clear plan for providing services, the problem that appears most urgent at the time is the one that gains the attention of a caring service provider. However the reactionary approach to service provision keeps organizations in crisis mode. This ever growing emergency status does not allow for the reflection, evaluation and capacity building that is needed to sustain an organization.

In order to develop an effective plan and process for meeting needs, the plan must begin with first identifying a single area of concern. The plan will be to eliminate the problem in those who are suffering rather than simply reducing the effects of a problem. The goal of eliminating a problem will help to target efforts towards the root causes of a problem.

For example, Mother Snow needed to stay committed to eliminating the problem of children being in the streets in harm's way. Then she could focus on her own ability by giving them access to her facility.   Her other efforts could have included finding ways to keep them properly supervised. Once she enlisted help, she could feel satisfied that her goal to eliminate the children's unsafe exposure to the streets was being met. She could feel confident that she provided a safe haven for a given number of children.

Once she has established her reputation in this single area of need, she will better understand what she requires in order to continue her success in that specific area. Then the other problems that arise can be addressed by *others* who specialize in those areas. These specialists will become partners who are committed to the same end result- meeting the needs of the clients to eliminate their problem.

Many of today's non-profit organizations are started by leaders who recognize problems that they want to eliminate. These leaders consider a problem to be significant enough to make it their mission to do whatever they can to eliminate it. Therefore a good *mission statement* first requires the recognition of a problem that needs to be eliminated.

An effective mission statement is concise, to the point, realistic, operational, inspirational, motivational, informative, and even emotional. It is not too abstract or even too intellectual. The mission clearly states the purpose of the organization. It is forward-thinking, positive, and describes success. It is clear and focused so that the reader can identify with the statement. It reflects the organization's values, and clearly enumerates the reasons why the organization exists. (Boardsource – http://www.boardsource.org)

A mission statement that includes the problem helps those who join the cause to stay focused upon solutions that are foundationally connected. At the same time if the problem changes then the mission may also change. It is very important that the mission is associated with a clearly defined problem in order to maintain direction within the organization. Therefore I believe that a *problem statement* should be determined even *before* a *mission statement* is developed.

TURNING PAIN INTO A PASSION FOR HELPING OTHERS

Mother Snow was a pillar in her community who dedicated herself to looking out for the protection of the children in her neighborhood. Her own children were adults when she started opening up her home as a safe haven. Mother Snow received comfort in knowing that she was offering protection for others. She began to experience her own healing in her helping others. She was not even concerned with whether the parents appreciated what she was doing. She knew that this was what was needed and she felt good about what she was doing.

Many compassionate people are abundant in their capacity to love. At the same time they may also have a great deal of experience in various areas of pain and suffering. My experiences with helping people learn the R.A.T.E.S. Principles have taught that most of our participants have had *multiple* tragedies in their lives. These experiences tend to compel them to have goals of helping to eliminate suffering in *several* areas. It is difficult for them to simply choose one specific focus to use while they learn how to build structure for their initiative. Just the possibility of being able to help someone overcome encourages them to want to attack all sorts of hardship.

At the same time, while they search for that one area of concern, they need to be encouraged that their pain and suffering is not a cause for shame and embarrassment. Those who are helped may even be comforted with knowing that their *helpers* can somehow relate to what they are experiencing. With this in mind, we should find ways to celebrate the fact that many service providers are *overcomers* who have journeyed through much suffering themselves. We should celebrate their decision to turn their pain into a passion for helping others.

1. What was Mother Snow's first objective?

_____

_____

_____

2. What other needs did she try to address?

_____

_____

_____

_____

3. Why did Mother Snow burn out?

_____

_____

_____

_____

4. What could Mother Snow have done before giving up on everything?

_____

_____

5. What could collaborative partners have done to support Mother Snows efforts?

_____

_____

_____

_____

HOW TO DETERMINE THE PROBLEM

A *service provider* is the entity that is responsible for providing services that lead to solving a problem. For the purposes of this material, we define a problem as something that causes pain, suffering or hardship. Problems to the extreme may also cause death. This death could be to a person, or even a healthy way of life.

It is important to recognize and believe that healing will begin and continue as people seek to eliminate the pain and suffering in the lives of others. When service providers seek to eliminate the pain and suffering that they have also experienced they have the ability to genuinely relate to those that they serve. This ability to relate helps to maintain the commitment as well as share in the healing.

The first *need* that service providers have is to determine *which* problem(s) they are committed and equipped to *eliminate*. By approaching a problem as one that is to be eliminated, the planning and resource gathering will be more focused and measurable. The qualifications for seeing success are clearer when success includes actual transformation from *wrong* to *right*.

Although the mindset of eliminating a problem is not the norm, it is essential for those who want to establish a lasting legacy. For example a service provider that has determined that unemployment is the primary problem will be guided to find a solution to eliminate unemployment. This mindset will force people to avoid wasted efforts on theories and practices that may not be goal oriented, measurable or result in success.

In R.A.T.E.S. workshops, we find that many people have an idea that something should be changed and that *they* want to do something about it. However, they tend to be clueless about what it would take to make the change that is needed. Because of this lack of understanding, many social and human service providers have launched projects that have only lasted long enough to spend the money and resources that were given to get started. At the same time, the mindset of *eliminating* a problem compels a person to think *long term* and to seriously consider the obstacles that may hinder their lasting success.

In order to decide upon the problems that you might be called to eliminate, first consider your thoughtful responses to the following question:

What pain, suffering or hardship have you experienced that you strongly desire to see eliminated?

This pain, suffering or hardship could be something that you experienced as a child or in later years. This could be something that someone else caused or experienced, but still resulted in your suffering.

For example if you suffered from alcoholism as an alcoholic, then you may list "alcoholism" as a problem. On the other hand, if you were a child of an alcoholic parent the problem still relates to alcoholism, but you might list the problem as an "alcoholic parent."

Both situations described above could result in directly causing pain, suffering or hardship. At the same time, even if you worked at a substance abuse clinic without ever having to experience direct personal addiction in some form, then alcoholism may not be an appropriate problem for you in this exercise. The reason is that your perspective as a service provider is not the same as one of a victim. Victims generally understand the challenges of a problem that they experience in ways that service providers often have difficulty grasping. This gap in understanding may be closed when the service provider is also a survivor from the hardship that is being serviced.

The "*Determine the Problems*" exercise used with teaching the R.A.T.E.S. Principles was developed to uncover heartfelt commitments to aid in launching an effective and solution driven organization. This exercise helps participants to look at their concerns objectively to help focus upon which issue is most pressing to them. This most pressing issue will be the concern that causes people to stick to their efforts even in the face of difficult challenges.

Generally people that have a personal stake and experience with a problem are more apt to stick with addressing it for a longer period of time. They find something that is fulfilling enough to do even without the need for outside appreciation. They would work to eliminate the problem without pay if needed. They would learn how to become experts in this area long enough to see some significant progress with doing away with this problem.

The *Determine the Problems* exercise requires participants to name their problems with short titles. Participants are required to restrict their problem titles to between one and three words. The purpose for limiting the description to between one and three words is because the resources for addressing those problems will be found quicker with short descriptive keywords. When searching for resources and information that can help to develop or sustain a project, knowing certain key words will help to narrow the search results. By narrowing the search results, you will be able to pinpoint solutions in less time.

Additionally, key words must be accompanied by descriptive narrations that expound upon the titles and headings. These narrations will help to paint a clearer picture about what is needed and why it is crucial to address the need. Drawing upon personal experiences helps to convince others that there is motivation to demonstrate success with eliminating a problem. It helps to build hope that there will be a reasonable show of commitment to the project.

There are several direct questions given with this exercise that will help to determine problem(s) that you may be committed to eliminate. A follow up exercise will set the platform for settling upon which problem should receive first priority for developing sound solutions. These exercises together help prepare the mindset needed to gain focus for structured, results oriented planning.

A) List up to five problems that have caused you pain and suffering in the spaces below. Do your best to use only 1 to 3 word descriptions. (Ex. Juvenile incarceration, Lack of employment)

1	2	3	4	5

For each of the problems listed, answer the following questions.

B) Do you feel that you have a responsibility to do something to stop this suffering?

C) Does this suffering bother you any time you hear about someone experiencing it?

D) How have you personally suffered from this problem while hoping that someone could have helped you?

E) Are you willing to work towards eliminating this problem for at least *3 years without pay* – if necessary? (While it is best that you get paid, this is about your *commitment*.)

Your answers to the previous questions will help to indicate how much you will be committed to addressing the problem that you will focus on eliminating.

Once a list of problems have been determined, it is necessary to settle upon the single problem that is to be addressed first. The rest of the problems may be dealt with later. However there needs to be an effort to first establish an area of expertise and targeted service. This will allow for concentrated skill building with regards to developing successful service delivery.

In order to help organize your efforts a Determine the Problem Table is provided. The First column is for listing up to five personal experiences that you believe are problems. The other five columns are designed to help participants determine if they have listed the types of problems that they could commit to addressing for a significant period of time.

The Focus on the Problem Worksheet will help to focus upon which problem will be addressed first. It is designed to examine the degree of commitment for each problem as they are individually compared to each other.

Follow these simple steps to determine a list of problems that you may be called to help eliminate in the lives of others.

Step 1: Make a list of up to 5 problems that you have overcome. Keep in mind that a problem is something that causes pain suffering or hardship. We must first admit that we have in fact pressed through situations that caused pain, suffering and hardship. For example, substance abuse is a problem. Unemployment could also be a problem. It could clearly be explained how each of those problems cause pain, suffering and hardship. Remember that your problems should be 1 to 3 word descriptions.

Step 2: Place your list of problems in the first column of the Determine the Problem table.

Step 3: Take the time to carefully consider the statements in the following columns. Place an "X" or check the spaces where the statement is true in regards to that particular problem.

Step 4: Circle the problems in the form that have 5 checks or X's. You will use these results for the next step. NOTE: If none of your problems have 5 checks, you are probably not committed to finding your calling at this time.

NOTE: See how the table is completed in the example below. Then use the blank table on the following page to determine the problems that you may select to eliminate.

Determine the Problems Table (*Example***)**

Place an X in the box(es) next to the problem where the statement is true.						
Problems (List the problems that you are compelled to address)	I strongly desire to eliminate this problem	This problem has caused me personal pain & suffering	I am personally responsible for doing something about this problem	It disturbs me to hear about someone else suffering from this problem	I would work to eliminate this problem WITH NO PAY	TOTALS
1 *unemployment*	X	X				2
2 *alcoholism*	X	X	X	X		4
3 *drunk driving*	X	X		X		3
4 *child abuse*	X	X	X	X	X	(5)
5 *juvenile incarceration*	X	X	X	X	X	(5)

Determine the Problems Table

Place an X in the box(es) next to the problem where the statement is true.						
Problems (List the problems that you are compelled to address)	I strongly desire to eliminate this problem	This problem has caused me personal pain & suffering	I am personally responsible for doing something about this problem	It disturbs me to hear about someone else suffering from this problem	I would work to eliminate this problem WITH NO PAY	TOTALS
1						
2						
3						
4						
5						

In order to narrow the focus (from the list developed from the Determine the Problems exercise), you will compare each problem against the others.

Step 1: Using your list from the previous step, write up to 5 problems in the boxes provided in the top of the form of the Focus on the problem sheet.

Step 2: For each row, compare the problems against each other. Imagine two people in front of you suffering from the problems being considered. Then decide which one of the problems you would be most compelled to address first. Mark the circle that represents the problem that you would address first.

Step 3: After comparing each problem (one row at a time) the circles under the problems are either marked "✓" or empty. Count the total number of marks, one column at a time, placing *that* total in the boxes provided below.

The total number of marks indicates the priority of importance when each problem is assessed objectively.

See the worksheet illustration.

Then use the blank form on the following page to complete the exercise for yourself. *In case of a tie, simply compare those against each other using the same criteria in Step 2.*

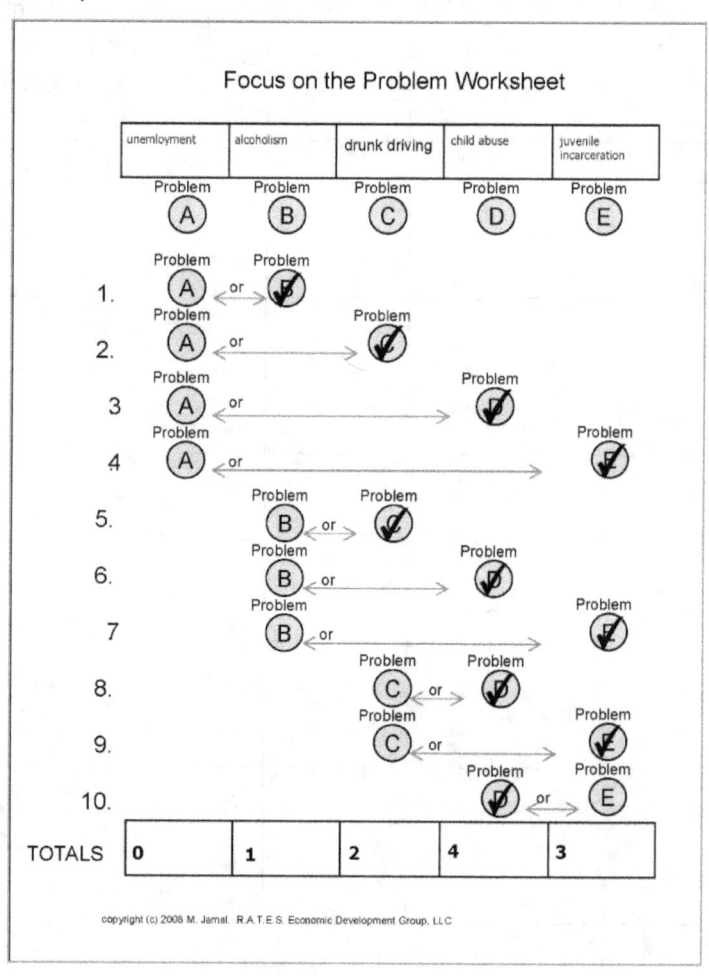

Focus on the Problem Worksheet

unemployment	alcoholism	drunk driving	child abuse	juvenile incarceration
Problem A	Problem B	Problem C	Problem D	Problem E

TOTALS

0	1	2	4	3

copyright (c) 2008 M. Jamal. R.A.T.E.S. Economic Development Group, LLC

Focus on the Problem Worksheet

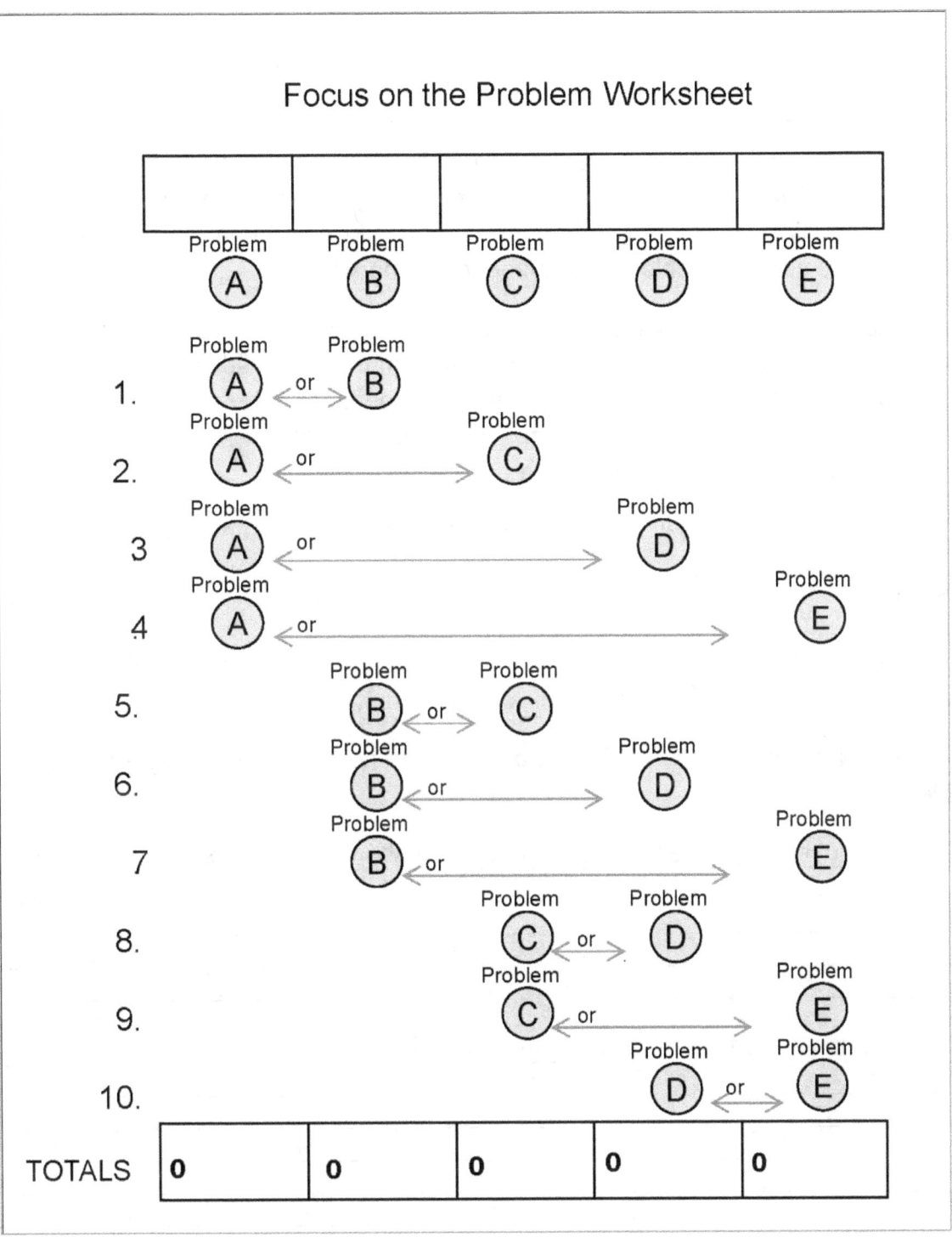

The Determine the Problem exercise can be completed in a group setting. Sometimes participants require help with describing their understanding of a problem. It is good to participate in a group exercise to further develop the ability to describe and fine tune a specific problem that will be the primary focus.

The members of the group will take turns describing characteristics and example experiences that occur with the primary problem that they have selected. The rest of the group will attempt to guess the short title of the problem based upon the description and explanation. The person explaining the problem is not allowed to use any of the keywords while explaining the problem to others.

NOTE: Remember *not* to say the keywords that were used in naming the problem.

DISCUSSION

After each member of the group has taken a turn describing his or her problem, the group will reflect upon how the exercise affected them.

Have each participant use the following questions to help with describing the problem:

1. How does this problem cause pain and/or suffering for others?

_____

_____

_____

_____

2. How has this problem caused *you* personal pain and/or suffering?

_____

_____

_____

_____

_____

DISCUSSION QUESTIONS TO CONSIDER *AFTER* THE GROUP EXERCISE

1) Were any of the participants challenged with describing the problem while being unable to use any of the key words? If so, why?

_____

_____

_____

2) Did any of the listeners agree with the presenter's descriptions after hearing the actual keywords title?

_____

3) Were any of the listeners able to contribute more descriptive explanations to help the presenter speak in more detail about the primary problem?

_____

4) What impressed the listeners about the presenters after hearing about each other's motivation for addressing a problem?

_____

_____

_____

5) Think about the problems that you believe you are called to eliminate. Why should you think about *eliminating* a problem rather than just trying to somehow "fix" it?

_____

_____

_____

When developing grant proposals or seeking donors, it is important to be able to explain why *you* are the one who should receive the resources for addressing a problem. People want to know that you have a real and personal stake in the success of a project or program. If you have no clear reason for your involvement, documented experience reveals that you are not as likely to stay committed when critical challenges arise.

THE NEEDS OF THE LEADERSHIP

NON-PROFIT LEADERSHIP NEEDS INFORMATION ABOUT RESOURCES

A primary need often expressed by non-profit leadership is to obtain adequate resources. Their typical complaint is about donors who offer small donations here and there while expecting that something major should be accomplished with it.

The people who can use the money to make a difference are generally not getting adequate funds. In fact, It is not unusual to see donors offer more money for *feasibility studies, advocacy* and *research* than for the actual efforts to service those in need. Then if a study indicates that they do not know how to solve the problem, the donors typically move on to fund something else without committing to supporting a solution.

The information about needed resources is generally available to those who have the savvy or expertise to do searches for the information. Unfortunately, those who have this expertise are generally not in the communities that have the problem.

NON-PROFIT LEADERSHIP NEEDS AFFIRMATION AND EMPATHY

The field of *Social Intelligence* seeks to aid in developing solutions to societal issues. Two primary components of Social Intelligence involve establishing an environment of Affirmation and Empathy.

My experience with supporting service providers revealed that these areas are critical when addressing their individual developmental needs. Many potential service providers display and express a need to be affirmed that their past pain, suffering and struggles have made them *better* able to care for others. This is important because leaders tend to shy away from open and honest assessments regarding their progress and challenges. They see their past struggles as stumbling blocks and blemishes to their otherwise success as survivors. This attitude towards their past hinders their ability to use their past experiences as a knowledge base for planning effective and practical solutions.

Sharing in intimacy and openness encourages participants to be empathetic with other leaders and service providers. This exercising of empathy sets a crucial foundation for true collaboration where the contributions of others will be better understood, encouraged and valued. Participants gain and enjoy a sense of supportiveness from their peers. Additionally, the leaders and providers also gain a deeper level of empathy for their potential clients during this process.

R.A.T.E.S. Principles emphasize the importance of focusing upon a specific area of interest. However the method for gaining this focus deals with the realization that it is best to start in an area with which there is personal stake for success. This attitude of being a stakeholder is vital to social service projects because human service delivery is risky and volatile. Those who have a personal stake in the success of a social service venture tend to offer greater commitment, even when the venture appears risky or presents barriers to its success.

For example, getting donors to offer enough support to fight breast cancer requires passionate and informed pleas for finances. One effective fundraising activity for health issues such as breast cancer is a walk-a-thon. The details that are required for planning a walk-a-thon include obtaining permits, soliciting volunteers, marketing, etc. Someone who has suffered with breast cancer may be more determined to press through all of the bureaucracy and expense for launching an awareness walk-a-thon than someone who has no personal experience with breast cancer at all.

Also my experience has uncovered that it is more difficult for service providers to abandon projects offering services that are birthed out of their own pain and suffering. This reluctance to quit makes those who have somehow suffered from a specific area of hardship better prospects for commitment to deliver continuous and practical solutions.

Those potential service providers who have suffered in their area of concern should not feel that they are less valuable because of their past experiences. Instead they should be celebrated as survivors with valuable insight that can lead to effective service delivery. They need to be affirmed that their experience will help mold the efforts and programs that are needed. In fact, their hardship experiences should be seen as events that can be used to strengthen and educate themselves and others.

Beginning with the Purpose and Mission

Before an organization can be assessed with regards to its ability to respond to the needs of clients, there should be a clear understanding of the organization's purpose and mission.   There must be clarity about why an organization exists in regards to the problem that it is committed to eliminate.

NON-PROFIT LEADERSHIP NEEDS TO DEFINE THE MISSION OF THEIR ORGANIZATION

There was a television series that was a big hit beginning in 1966. It had a trademark scene that would open up with a man receiving a clandestine message about an evil problem. This man would be told about the problem as well as who was causing the problem. He would also be told about some support that would be assigned to him if he decided to eliminate the problem.

This television series was called Mission Impossible. The series, which was created and initially produced by Bruce Geller, follows the missions of the Impossible Missions Force (IMF), a team of secret agents employed by the United States government. The team is sent on covert missions to combat dictators, evil organizations, and (primarily in later episodes) crime lords. (From Wikipedia, the free encyclopedia)

Just as in the series, a mission is always preceded by acknowledging that there is a problem needing to be addressed. A mission can be short termed or on-going according to the depth of the problem. The IMF specialized in short term missions that could have long term consequences. However the leader maintained an ongoing mission which was to eliminate evil threats to the United States. This is why the leader was always contacted about specific problems.

Your mission is what you have determined is the ultimate reason for your existence. Your mission statement expresses the primary vision that will continue to motivate you to persevere even if the budget is tight and the bills are overwhelming. Your mission is what gives your organization meaning. Your mission is ongoing when it involves eliminating a problem that causes pain and suffering for others.

A solid mission is fueled by a self-induced passion that produces it's own rewards - without needing the acknowledgement of others. In other words a lack of resources should not cause an organization to change the original mission. A lack of resources should compel an organization to find ways to address what is missing and acquire what is needed.

The capacity or ability to respond to the needs of the client must be in consideration of the organization's mission, and capability to adequately assess all resources that are available to the organization. The mission is a key element because it determines the consistency with which an organization performs its services. For example, an organization that has a mission to serve the housing needs of developing youth may agree to participate in a youth job fair project. However, when pressed with a shortage of time and resources may not continue with the job fair activities.

The job fair related activities could serve the youth, but could also serve another population outside of the mission focus. Depending upon the project, the partnering organization could then be faced with having to find resources to accommodate those non-youth participants. Responding to all the inquiries related to the job fair will require an expense of time and resources. The resources used for the job fair could deplete much of the needed resources that directly affect the intended population of youth. Therefore a job fair may not be a good project for a youth housing organization with little time and available resources.

Imagine that you are being offered $50,000 to launch a project. You will be limited to address only one need with this money on this first funding cycle. According to the success of this project, you will later receive twice as much money to expand this project. You will be judged initially on how well you respond to certain questions.

With the scenario above in mind answer the following questions:

1.   What primary problem do you feel most compelled to address? (Only one problem is allowed)

_____

_____

_____

2.   How does this problem affect those that you want to help?
For example: The problem of teen pregnancy contributes to juvenile poverty and child abandonment.

_____

_____

_____

_____

3. What will happen to those that you want to help if this problem is not addressed?
For example: Teen parents will increase the crime statistics, rate of homelessness and welfare recipients.

_____

_____

_____

_____

_____

4. Why do you feel that you have to be the one to address this problem?

_____

_____

a)   Why not just support someone else who does the same thing that you want to do?

_____

_____

_____

_____

5. What are some of the barriers or obstacles that could hurt your success with addressing this problem?

For example: Suppose your vision is to eliminate the number of high school drop outs is to offer a GED alternative. The potential participants may have poor study habits which could hinder your success with teaching them what they need in order to pass the GED exam. Therefore poor study habits could present barriers to the success of that project.

_____

_____

_____

_____

6. What makes you best qualified to address this problem?

_____

_____

_____

_____

a)   Why do you feel that you have to be the one to address this problem?

_____

_____

_____

_____

b)   What are some of the barriers or obstacles that could hurt your success with addressing this problem?

_____

_____

_____

_____

_____

_____

Service providers need to obtain adequate resources. This includes the human, material and financial resources that they need to eliminate problems. The human resources needed generally begin with basic support such as administration and additional service delivery staff. However, start-up non-profit leadership frequently underestimate the need for a Board of Directors that should include experts in key areas of concern.

Service providers need to unload the feelings of being overwhelmed with trying to solve problems. A good Board of Directors will help relieve the sense of being overburdened with having to run an organization alone. The Board of Directors that includes expertise in legal matters, accounting, fund raising and human resources will be a great asset to the leadership. This team will share the load in finding the resources that are needed. They will also offer their wealth of knowledge and influence.

However acquiring the commitment from such an array of skills and abilities is not an easy task. The founder or visionary has to convince potential board members that *their* needs are also being met. People who commit to serving as Board Members have a basic need to make a difference by contributing to the success of an organization. They also need to feel secure that they will not be held responsible for a failed or unsuccessful venture. Board members need to realize a reasonable return from their investment of time and other resources.

In his book, Ten Basic Responsibilities of Nonprofit Boards, Second Edition, Richard T. Ingram describes essential duties that should be expected of a Board of Directors. According to Mr. Ingram's book, board members are to, "Ensure adequate financial resources. One of the board's foremost responsibilities is to secure adequate resources for the organization to fulfill its mission." [1]

---

[1] Richard T. Ingram, Ten Basic Responsibilities of Nonprofit Boards, Second Edition (BoardSource 2009).

I believe that the Board of Directors are the first donors that a non-profit founder should work to acquire. They will bring their own sphere of resources to the effort once they have become committed. Together, they will help form a synergy that can insure consistent organizational achievements.

The Board of Directors provides the oversight of an organization. This board will offer direction to the primary leadership. The board members also provide support and encouragement for the one who is responsible for managing the organization. The primary makeup of a Board of Directors includes a Chair, Secretary and Treasurer. Each board member is responsible for making sure that the organization stays focused on achieving the stated goals. Board members also assume legal responsibility and liability for the conduct of an organization.

A good Board is able to respond to the funding needs of an organization through individual contributions as well as referrals and fund raising initiatives. Each board member must take on the responsibility of assuring that the organization remains solvent and productive. Board members are concerned with the fiscal as well as the program management of the organization.

Board members may also be divided into committees that concentrate on specific areas. These areas may include: a budget committee which oversees and approves the organizational and project budgets; an executive committee which addresses policies and legal agreements; a finance committee which is dedicated to making decisions about investments and fund raising activities; a public relations committee which is responsible for promoting and maintaining a good and inviting public image for the organization. A member of the board is selected to head each committee although each committee participant may not be an actual board member.

Board members should be selected according to how they will help meet the overall goals and objectives of an organization according to the stated mission. With this in mind, board members should have a vested interest in the carrying out the mission, goals and objectives of the organization. Therefore the makeup of board members should reflect the interest of the population that will be serviced according the organization's stated mission, goals and objectives. For example, an organization with a mission to service at-risk youth should include board members that have experience or a genuine interest with at-risk youth. The board membership should also include someone who has been an at-risk youth to gain a realistic perspective of the needs that should be addressed.

Since the board members are expected to address the fiscal management the board should include someone who is knowledgeable about finances and fund raising. A well rounded board should include members that are proficient in addressing each aspect of the mission statement, goals and objectives that are expressed by the organization. The ideal board of directors will also be able to address the organization's legal, financial, technical and resource concerns as well as provide moral support and encouragement for success.

Here is a sample developed by Rev. Edwin Perry for his non-profit that summarizes what an organization might submit to a potential board member.

As a potential Board member of Rev. H. Fort Feed My Sheep Food Pantry, we ask that you consider the following minimum expectations:

- ❖ Will bring knowledge and influence to help to move this organization to another level
- ❖ Help to oversee policies & procedures
- ❖ Help to raise funds
- ❖ Bring forth volunteers and other resources
- ❖ Help us to complete our projects
- ❖ Assist with fiscal oversight
- ❖ Help with the overall governance of the organization
- ❖ Serve as legal representative for contract approvals

In the table below write down names and occupations of people that you would consider as a board member according to each category of concern to your organization.

Area of Expertise	Name	Occupation/ Interest	Contact Information
Ex. Housing	John Doe	Construction Company Owner	303-555-7456 Johndoe@gmail.com

Non-profit leadership is also faced with many of the same challenges that for profit enterprises face. At the top of this list is adequate staff that help to support organizational goals.

The Bureau of Labor Statistics is a great resource for finding information about industries that provide services along with the positions and salaries. This includes non-profit industries. The BLS explains how nonprofits are different from for profit entities as follows: *These organizations span the political spectrum of ideas and encompass every aspect of human endeavor, from symphonies to little leagues, and from homeless shelters and day care centers to natural resource conservation advocates. These organizations often are collectively called "nonprofits," a name that is used to describe institutions and organizations that are neither government nor business. Other names often used include the not-for-profit sector, the third sector, the independent sector, the philanthropic sector, the voluntary sector, or the social sector. Outside the United States, these organizations often are called nongovernmental organizations (NGOs) or civil society organizations.*

These other names emphasize the characteristics that distinguish advocacy, grantmaking, and civic organizations from businesses and government. Unlike businesses, these organizations do not exist to make money for owners or investors, but that doesn't mean that they cannot charge fees or sell products that generate revenue, or that revenue must not exceed expenses. Instead, these groups are dedicated to a specific mission that enhances the social fabric of society. Unlike government, these organizations are not able to mandate changes through legislation or regulations enforceable by law. Instead, they work toward the mission of their organization by relying on a small group of paid staff and the voluntary service and financial support of large numbers of their members or the public. This industry includes four main segments: business, professional, labor, political, and similar organizations, civic and social organizations, social advocacy organizations, and grantmaking and giving services.[2]

Start up organizations are generally quite concerned about the type of personnel they should hire. Fortunately there are typical positions that seem to cross the spectrum of requirements even though the services may be varied. These positions that may be found in any non-profit organization include: Executive Director/ Chief Executive Officer, Program, Project Director, Program Aid, Secretary/ Administrative Assistant.

Besides knowing which positions to hire, non-profit leaders need to know how much each person should get paid. The next few pages will provide a brief job descriptions and salary range for each of the basic positions according to the Bureau of Labor Statistics.

---

[2] http://www.bls.gov/oco/cg/cgs054.htm

OCCUPATION:	EXECUTIVE DIRECTOR
Salary Range: ***Mean Weekly Hours***	46.9 hours
	Mean salary: $71,000-$160,000 per year

Job Description:

Determine and formulate policies and provide the overall direction of companies or private and public sector organizations within the guidelines set up by a board of directors or similar governing body. Plan, direct, or coordinate operational activities at the highest level of management with the help of subordinate executives and staff managers.

Perform a variety of duties depending on the size of their association and how it is organized. In a larger association, they may direct a number of operations specialty managers, each of whom is responsible for part of the organization's operations. In a small association, executives are likely to direct many or all of these functions themselves and be required to wear many hats at one time. Responsibilities include: overseeing planning, organizing, or coordinating the activities of a social service program or community outreach organization. They oversee the program or organization's budget and polices regarding participant involvement, program requirements, and benefits. Work may involve directing social workers, counselors, or probation officers and other staff.

OCCUPATION:	PROJECT DIRECTOR	
Salary Range:	***Mean Weekly Hours***	46.9 hours
	Mean Weekly Wage: **$1,077 per week**	
Job Description:		

Plans, directs, and coordinates activities of designated project to ensure that goals or objectives of project are accomplished within prescribed time frame and funding parameters: Reviews project proposal or plan to determine time frame, funding limitations, procedures for accomplishing project, staffing requirements, and allotment of available resources to various phases of project. Establishes work plan and staffing for each phase of project, and arranges for recruitment or assignment of project personnel. Confers with project staff to outline work plan and to assign duties, responsibilities, and scope of authority. Directs and coordinates activities of project personnel to ensure project progresses on schedule and within prescribed budget. Reviews status reports prepared by project personnel and modifies schedules or plans as required. Prepares project reports for management, client, or others. Confers with project personnel to provide technical advice and to resolve problems. May coordinate project activities with activities of government regulatory or other governmental agencies.

OCCUPATION:	PROGRAM DIRECTOR

Salary Range:	***Mean weekly Hours***	46.9 hours

Mean Weekly Wage: **$1,077 per week**

Job Description:

Manages program to ensure that implementation and prescribed activities are carried out in accordance with specified objectives: Plans and develops methods and procedures for implementing program, directs and coordinates program activities, and exercises control over personnel responsible for specific functions or phases of program. Selects personnel according to knowledge and experience in area with which program is concerned, such as social or public welfare, education, economics, or public relations. Confers with staff to explain program and individual responsibilities for functions and phases of program. Directs and coordinates personally, or through subordinate managerial personnel, activities concerned with implementation and carrying out objectives of program. Reviews reports and records of activities to ensure progress is being accomplished toward specified program objective and modifies or changes methodology as required to redirect activities and attain objectives. Prepares program reports for superiors. Controls expenditures in accordance with budget allocations. May specialize in managing governmental programs set up by legislative body or directive and be designated Manager, Governmental Program (government ser.).

OCCUPATION:	EXECUTIVE ASSISTANT

Salary Range:	**Mean Weekly Hours**	$ 41.2 hours

Mean Weekly Wage: **$1,014 per week**

Job Description:

Provides assistance to the Executive Director, including board activities, publications, volunteerism, and special events planning, to create and maintain favorable public image for the non-profit organization by performing the following duties:

Directs activities of organization to coordinate functions of various community health and welfare programs: Organizes and develops planning program to ascertain community requirements and problems in specific fields of welfare work, and to determine agency responsibility for administering program. Surveys functions of member agencies to avoid duplication of efforts and recommends curtailment, extension, modification, or initiation of services. Advises health and welfare agencies in planning and providing services based on community surveys and analyses. Reviews estimated budgets of member agencies. Prepares and releases reports, studies, and publications to promote public understanding of and support for community programs. May recruit and train volunteer workers. May organize and direct campaign for solicitation of funds. May visit agency sites to evaluate effectiveness of services provided.

OCCUPATION:	ADMINISTRATIVE ASSISTANT

Salary Range:	***Mean Weekly Hours***	40.8 hour
	Mean Weekly Wage: $1,079 per week	

Job Description:

Responsible for initiating and coordinating the clerical and secretarial functions required in effective implementation of administrative policies of a major academic or administrative unit. Responsible for directing the work of clerical employees in lower classifications.

Performs typing and transcription duties as required.

Establishes procedures that implement operational and/or fiscal policies.

Interprets policies and procedures as established by superiors.

Compiles data based on research techniques and on statistical compilations involving an understanding of operating unit programs, policies, and procedures.

Drafts financial, statistical, narrative, and/or other reports as requested.

Provides authoritative information that tends to establish precedents and which may commit a unit or superior to a policy or course of action.

Independently composes reports and correspondence containing decisions that tend to establish precedents and which may commit a unit or superior to a course of action.

Arranges, participates in, and implements, as directed, conferences and committee meetings.

Coordinates the activities of, and provides semiprofessional service to, university committees. Signs in behalf of superior, as delegated, his or her name to correspondence, requisitions, vouchers, and other forms of consequence.

Performs related duties as assigned.

Knowledge, Skills, and Abilities:

Ability to accurately deal with difficult dictation. Ability to perform difficult typing duties. Administrative ability. Supervisory ability. General administrative review of objectives is provided by a designated administrator.

OCCUPATION:	PROGRAM AIDE

Salary Range:	*Mean Weekly Hours*	41.2 hours

Mean Weekly Wage: **$1,014 per week**

Job Description:

Leads group work activities, as directed by agency program staff: Receives instructions from Program Director, Group Worker prior to initiating group activities. Plans program details to meet needs and interests of individual members. Interests participants in various activities, such as arts and crafts and dramatics. Demonstrates techniques for active sports, group dances, and games. Helps develop new skills and interests. May work with part-time or volunteer staff.

COMMON ORGANIZATIONAL DUTIES

Here is a simple summary of some common duties that may need to be performed by an organization for a particular project:

- Locate and secure a facility
- Recruit clients
- Complete entry or intake documents
- Maintain client records
- Bill the client
- Maintain payroll
- Supervise the staff

Can you think of other duties that might be needed?

Use the table below to organize assigning the type of staff member that might be best suited to perform and complete each task. For example the Project Director might be assigned to "Locate and secure a facility" because he or she has a good idea about that space needed to complete the project.

STAFF DUTIES TABLE

Activity	Responsible Staff member	Resources needed to effectively complete the task (supplies, facility, equipment, assisting staff)
Directs and coordinates activities of project personnel to ensure project progresses on schedule and within prescribed budget.		
Drafts financial, statistical, narrative, and/or other reports as requested. Performs typing and transcription duties as required.		
Plans and develops methods and procedures for implementing program, directs and coordinates program activities, and exercises control over personnel responsible for specific functions or phases of program.		

THE NEEDS OF THE CLIENT

Before assembling a staff for service delivery, the non-profit leadership needs to be clear about what they plan to do to eliminate problems as well as *who* they plan to serve.

After focusing upon a specific problem to eliminate, a target population needs to be established. Your target population is also referred to as your *consumers* or *clients*. The client is anyone who makes use of your services. As you continue to build your organization, it will be to your advantage to understand and adapt a very important phrase that we pass on to all of our students. That phrase is, "*Everybody is not my client.*" There may be many different people who fit your client profile according to your target population. However until they agree that they need you and agree to use your services to eliminate their problems, they are not your clients, although they may be your target population.

Any effort to eliminate a problem needs to identify tangible beneficiaries of its success. Selecting a target population is important, because it helps to focus the program development. It also helps to build the tools for measuring success.

Program development is the process of planning what will be done on behalf of the clients to provide services. A *good* service program includes developing a series of activities that work together to produce a measure of improvement. The measured success will be contingent upon the feedback that is documented through the client.

Since the way people may respond to program delivery varies from person to person, a client profile will help determine any patterns of effectiveness. For example, a program that offers education about *Encore Careers* may receive greater participation from elderly men (age 50-65) than from younger men (age 18-26). In this case, the program may be considered more effective for men between the ages of 50 and 60.

Establishing a target population needs to be done with great thought and consideration. In some situations, the target population is established with the vision.

An example of this is the Young Women's Christian Association, commonly referred to as the WYCA. – The WYCA was formed in London by Emma Robarts and Mrs. Arthur Kinnaird in 1855.

The YWCA movement was introduced to the United States with New York City and Boston opening women's residences in 1858. The target population for the YWCA is indicated in their formal mission statement which is as follows: The YWCA USA is a women's membership movement nourished by its roots in the Christian faith and sustained by the richness of many beliefs and values. Strengthened by diversity, the YWCA draws together members who strive to create opportunities for women's growth, leadership, and power in order to attain a common vision: peace, justice, freedom, and dignity for all people. The YWCA will thrust its collective power toward the elimination of racism, wherever it exists, and by any means necessary.

Their mission statement demonstrates an example that supports the previous lesson for focusing on eliminating a specific problem. According to their mission statement, the problem that the YWCA is committed to eliminate is racism. At the same time they also indicate a target population that they clearly plan to support, which are young women. With the target population so well defined, it is easy for the YWCA to plan intervention activities and evaluation plans. It is also easier to research potential donors who want to help their target population.

Many new non-profit organizations begin with the idea that they want to help *any*one and *everyone*. While this is a noble posture, attempting to serve anyone and everyone is a sure way to lose sight of how effective your services may be. Organizations that have the most difficulty getting and maintaining clients include those who have not taken the time to adequately profile the type of people who would want, need and appreciate their services.

When people seek services who have needs other than what you have to offer, they will quickly conclude that your services are bad and not beneficial to them – or for anyone else. Unfortunately, *unqualified* clients also tend to conclude that your reason for not helping them is because you simply have a poorly run organization. Organizations that have not identified their target population maintain a high probability for mounting numerous complaints from dissatisfied clients.

A worksheet entitled "Who's Your Client?" is included in this writing to help you to establish your target population. This will address the question of who will benefit from your being successful with eliminating the problem. You will also narrow the focus even more to describe the type of people that you are committed to serve. You will not be able to effectively assess client needs until after you have first identified your clients.

The *Who's Your Client* worksheet will connect the results of the earlier lesson by developing a profile of the clients who will benefit from eliminating the pain and suffering. This process will answer the questions such as:

1) Who benefits from this problem being eliminated.

2) And Who is the target population?

You are going to use the *Who's Your Client* worksheet to help you to:

- select specific target population characteristics.

- determine what types of people suffer with the problem being addressed by this project.

- provide reasoning for the type of population that you choose for each category.

NOTE: You do not have to use every category in this list. You may also add categories of your own.

Who's Your Client
Profile Summary Worksheet

The Primary Problem that I am committed to eliminating is:_____

The Client profile of my target population includes the following:

Personal Characteristics (age range, gender, ethnic background, etc.)

_____   _____   _____

_____   _____   _____

Social Challenges (ex–offender, unemployed, etc.)

_____   _____   _____

_____   _____   _____

Geographic location

City:_____   State:_____

Zip/Postal Code:_____   County:_____

Ward:_____   Precinct:_____

Congressional District:_____   Senatorial District:_____

Region:_____   Country:_____

Population:_____   Unemployment Rate:_____

Poverty Rate:_____   Crime Rate:_____

Other stats (explain):_____

Now that you have settled upon a problem to eliminate and have also developed a client profile of your target population, it's time to plan your response to your client needs. The needs that concern you should be restricted to those needs that result from having the problem that you are committed to eliminating. For example, if your client needs housing, but the lack of housing does not influence the problem that you are eliminating, then the need for housing will not be your concern. However if the lack of housing hinders your ability to service your client, then this need should be factored into your options for possible solutions to your client's problem.

In the previous sessions you first determined a primary problem to eliminate. Then you identified a profile of the type of people who suffer from the problem that you plan to eliminate. Response-ability is having and demonstrating the ability to give a favorable response to needs. Whatever response you plan to give should be in consideration of what your target population or client needs in order to get relief from his or her problem. However your organization must consider, along with the client needs, the needs of your staff, partners, donors and the organization as a whole. You first settled upon the primary problem that you are committed to eliminating. Then you developed a profile of the characteristics of the people who have this problem. These are the people who will receive your services.

It is essential to ask yourself the question, "what does my client need in order to *not* have to *suffer* from the problem that I am committed to eliminating?" Although the response to this question is crucial, this may not be an easy question to answer. At the same time, it is even more difficult to answer for anyone who has not suffered from the problem at all. This is why the *Determine the Problem* exercise is so important to work through honestly. In addition the *Who's Your Client* exercise was important to help plan focused and targeted services that will provide a favorable response to client needs.

Ultimately, clients need to have their problems eliminated. They also need to have *hope* to hold on and persevere as they seek the help that they need in order to eliminate the problem.

The people that have suffered from the problem that you are committed to eliminating have a need for services that will lead to overcoming that problem. Your client needs to feel a sense of relief from the pain and suffering caused by that problem.

There are two primary issues that must be considered in order to provide successful solutions to societal problems. The first issue is whether or not solving the particular problem will eliminate the pain and suffering that has been identified. The second issue is whether or not the target population *agrees* that the problem stated is the problem that they want to eliminate. This second issue is one of the reasons that preparing a good needs assessment is critical.

After you have settled upon a problem to eliminate and have also developed a client profile of your target population, it's time to plan your response to your client needs. The needs that concern you should be restricted to those needs that result from having the problem that you are committed to eliminating. For example, if your client needs housing, but the lack of housing does not influence the problem that you are eliminating, then the need for housing will not be your concern. However if the lack of housing hinders your ability to service your client, then this need should be factored into your options for possible solutions to your client's problem.

Whatever response you plan to give should be in consideration of what your target population or client needs in order to get relief from his or her problem.

In some cases you may be compelled to advocate on behalf of your client because the standard treatments simply do not work. This may especially be a concern for those receiving government funds or grants from rigid donors. You may have to be innovative in how you meet the needs of your clients while still meeting the requirements of the donor.

For example a person with the problem of substance abuse that has gainful employment may not be in need of vocational training. It could be a waste your client's valuable time to force him or her to participate in vocational training simply because it is a requirement for your program. However there may be a module in your vocational training that includes a highly effective personality assessment. You can then focus on the personality assessment portion of the vocational training while still satisfying program requirements. This might help keep you from having a disgruntled client.

If your client expressed a need to have better communication and acceptance in the workplace, the personality assessment tool could be used to identify communication deficiencies. In this case the specific section that addresses the personality assessment should be what is made available to your client without forcing the entire vocational training service. When an organization designs solutions that are specific to the particular problems of a client, there is a greater likelihood that the client will willingly and successfully engage in the program activities.

Your solution to the problem should be designed to address the specific needs that arise from that problem. For example, imagine that you have a client who suffers from drug addiction that is also a homeless veteran, with other health problems. In this example, the problem that you are committed to eliminate is only substance abuse. However, a homeless client is difficult to keep engaged with services due to challenges associated with unstable housing.

The stress of not having stabile housing may hinder the treatment services from lasting, because your client is self medicating the stressful feelings with drugs. The health issues may also contribute to doctors prescribing medications that trigger the desire for narcotics.

I am aware of an example of a doctor that prescribed the drug Vicodin for a client that had been in a drug recovery program. This client had remained free from heroin use for over 4 years. The feelings that occurred with the Vicodin drug triggered a desire to maintain the euphorically numbing feeling that heroin once provided. After the Vicodin bottle was emptied this person went back into the streets in search of heroin. In this example, an evaluation of the services may have declared the recovery program to be ineffective.

DISCUSSION

What additional needs should have been considered for the client in the example above?

_____

_____

_____

_____

PURPOSE FOR CLIENT NEEDS ASSESSMENTS

A needs assessment will help to determine the nature and severity of the problem that is being eliminated for your clients. Without knowing the nature and impact of the problem, it is impossible to decide how to eliminate it. Data from the needs assessment can also help to gain support and resources for prevention and intervention projects.

A baseline needs assessment provides knowledge of client related conditions before engaging in a project or program. This type of assessment is a necessary first step in conducting an evaluation of a program's effectiveness. When a baseline assessment is given to a client before introducing a new activity, it is easier to monitor and record the extent that a problem has declined.

A growing number of social entrepreneurs are coming to terms with the reality that treating symptoms rather than addressing underlying causes has resulted in a tremendous waste of resources. They are being encouraged to maximize resources by targeting efforts where they will make the greatest impact. They are also aware that the problem is not always obvious.

When planning a needs assessment, it should first be clear how the assessment will be used. For example, if a needs assessment will be used to develop the program activities then there may be more open ended questions. Open ended questions are questions that allow the respondent to give an answer that was not included in the document. An example of an opened question is, "What services have you requested that you did not receive?"

However, if the needs assessment is mainly to measure the client's perspective of how much a service is needed, the questions may include rating numbers. The following is an example of a rating question:

The service that you received was delivered in a timely fashion.

☐4 Strongly Agree | ☐ 3 Agree | ☐ 2 Disagree | ☐ 1 Strongly Disagree

The results of a needs assessment will help to design the type of intervention and or prevention activities and resources for developing a program

Examine the **Needs Assessment Planning Form** on the following page to see how to list hardships that are caused by, or result from the problem that you are committed to eliminate. This list will be used to allow potential clients to influence the type of services that will be offered to them.

The Needs Assessment Planning Form illustration demonstrates planning the needs for people suffering with substance abuse. Notice that the first related problem is homelessness. This issue has its own set of needs to address.

Example

Primary problem of: *substance abuse*

The problem that I plan to eliminate causes my client to suffer with: *homelessness*

Therefore (he/ she) has a need for
1) *housing assistance*
2) *transitional housing options*
3) *housing vouchers to cover rent*

Primary problem of :

The problem that I plan to eliminate causes my client to suffer with:

therefore (he/ she) has a need for:
1)
2)
3)

The problem that I plan to eliminate causes my client to suffer with:

therefore (he/ she) has a need for:
1)
2)
3)

RESPONSE-ABILITY EXERCISE

When preparing to offer a favorable response to client needs it is important to have the tools to assess available resources.   A lack of resources will challenge the organization's ability to provide a response that make clients feel that their needs are met. This exercise will help a thought process to plan favorable responses to client needs.

RESPONDING TO THE NEEDS OF THE CLIENT

1.   Describe your client? What type of population are you called to serve? Be as specific as you can. (ex. Unemployed, Minority women that have been incarcerated and have children in poverty)

_____

_____

_____

_____

_____

2.   What are you prepared to offer these clients in your proposed project?

_____

_____

_____

_____

3.   What are the overall needs of these clients?

_____

_____

_____

_____

_____

_____

4.   What client needs will *not* be addressed by your project (because they fall *outside* of your mission focus)?

_____

_____

_____

_____

5.   How will your client's unmet needs affect your ability to serve your clients?

_____

_____

_____

_____

6. What organizations do you know that can address your clients' needs that are outside of your mission focus? Use the table below to organize your information:

UNMET CLIENT NEED	POTENTIAL SERVICE PROVIDER

HANDLING CLIENT COMPLAINTS

Organizations should have a standard for handling complaints from clients. These standards may be contained in a document called "Organization Policies and Procedures."   The reason that organizations have a document of policies and procedures is because there you or your staff will not be tempted to respond in a prejudicial way. It also protects the organization from being accused of discriminatory practices.

EXERCISE ROLE PLAYING

Role-playing is an effective method for preparing responses to client complaints. Active role-playing helps to reveal some character development that may be needed by staff in order to handle potentially hostile confrontations with clients.

Practice role-playing your response to client complaints by making up situations that have occurred or that you think might happen one day.

Scenario Example1 : Mr. Mad calls about a need for your service, but does nor meet your eligibility requirement. You need to explain to him that he is not eligible and then provide him with an alternative. However Mr. Mad insists that he is eligible and that you are just discriminating against him.

Scenario Example 2: Ms. Led insists that you enroll her daughter into your program, but you are already filled to capacity. She pleads with you that she has tried every other option and now your organization is the last hope left. After explaining to Ms. Led that you have already maximized the capacity you allow her daughter in your program. However a few weeks later Ms. Led complains that her daughter is not receiving enough attention to her needs.

DISCUSSION

1. How do you respond to a client that has expressed that you or your organization has not met his or her need? (Pretend that you have a client that complains about getting the wrong service from a member of your staff. Act out how it should be handled.)

2. Why should an organization take the time to respond to a grievance made by a client? (Pretend that a client brings a complaint to you at a time that you are much busier than usual and you are trying to meet a deadline for an audit. Act out how it should be handled.)

A primary component of *Response-ability* is having the ability to give a *favorable* response to *staff* or *personnel* needs. The staff includes all of those who share the tasks for providing effective services on behalf of an organization. The goals and objectives that an organization establishes for serving their clients will dictate the specific staffing needs.

One of the greatest and often overlooked need for the staff is *staff development,* including *Technical Training, Effective Client Relationships* and *Team Building.* The technical training will allow personnel to stay abreast of their field of employment and become confident in their service delivery. Team building will help the staff to remain supportive of each other which builds a stronger workforce. And instruction regarding Effective Client Relations will empower the staff to remain the type of service providers who gain a reputation for exceptional client satisfaction.

Consider the following scenario: A middle aged man enters the door of a recovery support program especially developed for people who have been incarcerated and have substance abuse issues. This man informs an receptionist at the front desk that he has never been arrested, but smokes a little marijuana. He states that the reason that he has come to this organization is because he needs a job. He had heard that this program helped ex-offenders to get jobs. Upon further inquiry the receptionist learns that this man has a resume and work experience that could help him easily qualify for a position that was recently posted.

While this program has an objective to help people to get jobs, they have a mandate and responsibility to find jobs for certain types of people. They are being funded to find employment specifically for former prison inmates who have had substance abuse issues.

It might be easier for the organization to place this man in employment, because he is not hindered by the stigma of being an ex-offender. However if this man fills the position, then there would be one less opportunity to have it filled by a true client for this program.

The dilemma described in the passage above is played out in many organizations. The staff is often faced with their desire to help, along with their obligation to work within certain guidelines. A dedicated employee may seek to be a problem solver for clients, but have trouble distinguishing a qualified client from a potential client.

A qualified client is one that has been assessed and found to fit the required profile for receiving services. A qualified client has the required problems, needs and background that the program is designed to accommodate.

Many organizations have difficulty with indoctrinating their staff and support regarding the treatment of only *qualified* clients. Likewise many workers are simply not certain about when or if they are able to go beyond the given criteria for participation. For this reason, organizational leaders will do well to establish clear and readily understood guidelines for identifying a client.

DISCUSSION

1. Should a staff member pass on employment information to a *non*-client or should this information be kept to share only with clients meeting criteria for services in the program?

_____

_____

_____

_____

_____

2. How could this situation impact the needs of the leadership, client and staff?

_____

_____

_____

_____

_____

_____

Many non-profit personnel encounter clients with a bundle of issues that they may consider to be problems even though they are only *symptoms* of the real problem. Social service providers have to be able to identify the problems that need to be addressed even above the distress of other issues that may only appear to be the problem.

For example, a group of community activists expressed their dissatisfaction with the city's decision to build a golf course in an area where the schools had been on academic probation. Not having enough golf courses in public schools was hardly viewed as a problem. The community residents could not see what golfing had to do with reading and math scores.

Community studies and surveys by an independent community organizer revealed that this particular school had a problem with attracting quality teachers. Good teachers were discouraged from teaching at the school because the surroundings were so gloomy and ghetto ridden. The golf course would give the appearance of a more upscale and productive environment. Teachers could be more willing to participate in a progressive project rather than what at first appeared to be a failing effort.

The R.A.T.E.S. position is that if people would take the initiative to engage in their calling, we can close the gap of need versus solution. We will have much less situations where organizations are over taxed and overburdened with trying to go beyond their capabilities.

Each organization needs to assess its own abilities to respond to the needs of those they are called to serve. The success of an organization begins when people who seek after their services agree that their needs are being met. People will continue to revisit an organization once the organization has demonstrated the ability to respond to their needs.

Staff members need to first determine a problem before assessing the solutions that would eliminate it. Once the problem has been determined, any number of solutions may appear valid.

It may be tempting to settle for making the problem a little less burdensome by addressing the *symptoms*. However, simply treating the symptoms may actually worsen the underlying problems. What happens too often is that a great amount of time, effort, and resources are wasted on symptoms. Consequently, by the time the problem is revisited the resources have been depleted.

A growing number of social entrepreneurs are coming to terms with a reality that treating symptoms rather than addressing underlying causes has resulted in a tremendous waste of resources. They are being encouraged to maximize resources by targeting efforts where they will make the greatest impact. At the same time they are aware that the problem is not always obvious.

There was a boy (call him Ted) in our after school program who got into trouble because he was acting out. The other youth told on him and the youth worker sent him to me claiming that he had a behavior problem. I was surprised to hear about this behavior which he had not displayed before.

It was relatively easy to calm Ted down, but I decided to get to the bottom of his issue since this was clearly out of character for him. I sat him down and asked him what he was doing. After some probing, he informed me that he was "acting crazy." Upon further questioning he let me know that his mother taught him how to act crazy so that he can get money.

Ted was hoping that his behavior would get him some money. For this boy his bad behavior was a means to get money. However his actions gave no indication that his problem was a lack of money. In his mind the best way to solve his money problem was to fake craziness. At the same time if I had not learned about his concern he might have decided that he did not act crazy enough to get the money. This could have prompted him to do something crazy enough to have gotten him dismissed from the program.

Ted did not understand that the crazy act was only reserved for the social worker and mental health counselor. Since his mother had not coached him to keep this act a secret from others he was glad to let me know about his skills as an actor. That day after the program, he had to go home with the same problem of empty pockets.

DISCUSSION

1.   What problem did Ted have? _____
_____
_____

2.   What symptoms did Ted show that pointed to his problem? _____
_____
_____
_____

3.   What could have been done to *eliminate* Ted's problem? _____
_____
_____
_____

4.   What is the difference between a *symptom* and a *problem*? _____
_____
_____
_____
_____
_____

5.   Is poverty a *symptom* or a *problem*? (Explain your answer.) _____
_____
_____
_____
_____

Response-ability considers the organization's ability to respond to the need for services as well as the staff's ability to perform the duties needed. In addressing personnel Response-ability, organizations need to assess the appropriate human resources required to provide quality service. However, in order to assess what staffing is needed, the organization must prepare detailed list of duties that must be performed for a project or program. This same information will be used to generate job descriptions and performance evaluations.

PARTNER NEEDS

If the leadership of an organization desires maximum input from the staff, they should elevate them to partners. A partner takes ownership while a staff worker takes a job. In order to get real contributions from the "partners" there are needs that they have which should be considered. Partners need:

• to feel like their input to eliminate a problem matters.

• to know that they will be in the loop with the flow of information.

• to feel that they will be included with making decisions that affect them.

• to know that they will be encouraged to take action and chances.

• to know that they will be supported ,even through the mistakes.

The list above for partners alternates between knowing and feeling certain ideas. This is because although something may be stated and even written as policy, if partners do not feel the commitment from leadership, they may not trust in what is written *or* stated.

When recruiting partners to form collaborative efforts, remember that they also have fundamental needs in order to maintain a working partnership. Your efforts to give a favorable response to those needs can greatly enhance your capability to deliver relevant services without experiencing burn out. The word collaboration contains the words "co" and "labor" indicating that there will be entities laboring together. You and your collaborators will labor or work together towards common results.

The ability to collaborate effectively will allow projects to work better because it relieves the burden of trying to meet all of the needs alone. People can plan and respond much better when they feel that they have the help and resources that they need. Collaboration offers a sense of empowerment through shared responsibility.

ORGANIZATIONAL NEEDS

Organizational needs include: adequate facility, adequate staffing, effective leadership, opportunity for growth and expansion along with appropriate financial support. The leadership of an organization is crucial and will determine the organization's ability to sustain and even expand.

The Board of Directors provides the oversight of an organization. This board will offer direction to the primary leadership. The board members also provide support and encouragement for the one who is responsible for managing the organization.   The primary makeup of a Board of Directors includes a Chair, Secretary and Treasurer. Each board member is responsible for making sure that the organization stays focused on achieving the stated goals. Board members also assume legal responsibility and liability for the conduct of an organization.

A good Board is able to respond to the funding needs of an organization through individual contributions as well as referrals and fund raising initiatives. Each board member must take on the responsibility of assuring that the organization remains solvent and productive. Board members are concerned with the fiscal as well as the program management of the organization.

Board members may also be divided into committees that concentrate on specific areas. These areas may include: a budget committee which oversees and approves the organizational and project budgets; an executive committee which addresses policies and legal agreements; a finance committee which is dedicated to making decisions about investments and fund raising activities; a public relations committee which is responsible for promoting and maintaining a good and inviting public image for the organization. A member of the board is selected to head each committee although each committee participant may not be an actual board member.

Board members should be selected according to how they will help meet the overall goals and objectives of an organization according to the stated mission. With this in mind, board members should have a working knowledge and understanding of the initial vision, problem and needs that are being addressed. Additionally, the makeup of board members should reflect the interest of the population that will be serviced according the organization's stated mission, goals and objectives. For example, an organization with a mission to service *at-risk youth* should include board members that have experience or a genuine interest with *at-risk youth*. The board membership should also include someone who has been an *at-risk youth* to gain a realistic perspective of the needs that should be addressed.

Since the board members are expected to address the fiscal management the board should include someone who is knowledgeable about finances and fund raising. A well rounded board should include members that are proficient in addressing each aspect of the mission statement, goals and objectives that are expressed by the organization. The ideal Board of Directors will also be able to address the organization's legal, financial, technical and resource concerns as well as provide moral support and encouragement for success.

THE NEEDS OF THE DONOR

In human and social services, a problem that is most urgent is one that results in pain, suffering or even death. Today's service providers work diligently to become a priority for funding by expressing how their concern requires urgent attention. Those who clearly justify the time, resources and expense to eliminate an urgent problem are the ones that generally get funded.

Proactive donors understand that problems causing pain and suffering have a negative influence on productivity. Most have an idea that production tends to stop when pain and suffering abound. Many donors also realize that when production stops, then extinction is imminent. Perhaps this is a reason that many donors seek to fund those organizations that clearly demonstrate the ability to produce results.

A person who is about the *business* of eliminating human pain and suffering is a *social entrepreneur*. The term *social* is from the word "*society*", which comes from the Greek *socius*, which means "*sharing.*" *Entrepreneur* comes from the word "*enterprise.*" It is a French word that means to "*to take action, take risks, and responsibility.*" A social entrepreneur takes action with getting people to share for the good of those in need.

At the same time, someone who makes it her or his business to help others out of love for humanity is a *charitable* entrepreneur. Charity comes from the Greek word caritas, meaning "love." Although all social entrepreneurs may not be charitable entrepreneurs, all charitable entrepreneurs are social entrepreneurs.

Today's Human Service providers have to become savvy *social* entrepreneurs who are able to find donors with the heart of *charitable* entrepreneurs. They have to learn how to establish relationships that capitalize on the reality that the service provider and donors are all entrepreneurs. Everyone is taking a risk when seeking to serve those who are experiencing pain, suffering and hardship. A smart service provider must learn to understand and *appreciate* that donors also take risks when they give to charitable efforts.

However, few service providers recognize that potential donors have their own needs. Donors have many different reasons for giving. A representative from a money management firm once told me that in his years of experience he saw two great motivators for the wealthy to give. He said one is *fear* and the other is *greed*. I somewhat understood the fear, but needed more clarity with how greed could prompt a wealthy person to give. He explained that if donors can see how their giving can increase their own wealth in tax deductions or favors (directly or indirectly) they can be convinced to make considerable donations.

I was relieved to meet someone who formed an organization that would encourage yet another reason to give, which is genuine love and caring for the welfare of others. This man is J.T. Dock Houk who was mentioned earlier. He started the National heritage Foundation in 1968 to allow people with a heart to help others to test their vision for change. His writings reflect someone on a mission to change the thinking of those wealthy individuals who have the ability to alleviate human suffering, but for some reason choose not to contribute. He also passionately promotes empowering those who may feel insignificant to realize that everyone can have a place in making the world better.

It has sometimes been difficult to research and uncover the vast wealth that exists while also researching the fixable suffering that also exists. There are so many hurting children who are looking to us and saying "fix it." Yet there are many enabled individuals and organizations in our world that have seemingly turned their heads away from the problems. Some have expressed that they did not see how their contribution could make a difference. R.A.T.E.S. is designed to help donors partner with those who are also partnering with others to make a measurable and accountable difference.

Dock Houk once made a statement in a seminar that we sponsored which had a profound effect on me. He stated that he felt that we needed to "find ways to minister to the donor." That is when I realized that donors also have needs. Donors need to feel confident that they are investing in an organization that will prove their ability to improve the lives of those who suffer from the problem being eliminated. Donors also need :

- to know that their donations are being given to good stewards.

- to feel like their donations are investments that have a lasting positive impact on eliminating a problem.

- to feel like their contributions (however small) will be appreciated.

- to feel like an organization is not solely dependent upon them to sustain their efforts.

Donors also need our prayers and encouragement. They need to be view as much more than a paycheck. Donors are also partners who have a stake in the success of whatever initiative that they support.

Account-ability is having and demonstrating the ability to account for program and fiscal activities and associated resources. It takes into consideration the systems that are in place to account for and track what is actually going on in an organization.

Accountability is really about stewardship. One day my husband (and partner), Rev. Dr. Aaron Jamal and I were discussing a situation that concerned me a little more than usual. I said to my husband, "It appears that most of these organizational leaders do not like to be disciplined." And he responded to me with something that tugged at my thoughts for a bit. He said that, "it is not so much about *liking* to be *disciplined* as it is about *allowing* yourself to be *accountable*."

Some of the areas that non-profit organizations typically need to account for include the following: 1) The type and number of people that are serviced. 2) Money received, Money spent, 3) Other Resources received 4) Resources used 5) Assets that are recognized 6) Appreciation or depreciation of assets 7) Time contributed by paid staff 8) Time contributed by non-paid staff 8) Compliance with IRS reporting (990/ 990 PF, W2, W4). This is not an exhaustive list, but gives an idea about what organizations should be able to track.

A report on a 2002 National Conference for Grantmakers provided some notable insight regarding how they will approach future donations and non-profit support. The entire report gives evidence that funders are requiring a greater degree of accountability than before. Specifically with regards to accountability the following was stated by Paul C. Light, who is the author of *Pathways to Nonprofit Excellence*, "The events of September 11 ushered in a new reality for nonprofits, according to Light. On one hand, the attacks and their aftermath brought an immediate surge in charitable giving and a dramatic increase in public confidence in government and civic institutions. However, at the same time, controversies concerning the disbursement of September 11-related funds by the American Red Cross and the United Way resulted in a media outcry about the ability of nonprofits to spend money wisely and in accountability ways.

'Performance, not promises, is the currency of public trust today, which means that organizational effectiveness has never been more important,' Light said."

If something great happened that inspired the public to all of a sudden begin giving your organization massive donations for you to distribute to other organizations, how would you account for the funds?

_____

_____

_____

_____

_____

_____

_____

_____

What system would you put in place to provide the ability to handle and account for the diverse distributions required?

_____

_____

_____

_____

_____

_____

_____

_____

_____

_____

_____

Today's grant makers are concerned with the ability of a nonprofit organization to hold itself accountable. There are various areas of accountability that may be required. However, the experience that I have had with both government and private funding has resulted in our learning to stay prepared to document account-ability in the following areas:

❑ Recording good Board meeting minutes

❑ Recruitment activities (newspaper ads –receipts, copies, flyers)

❑ Participant Enrollee Roster (dated with contact information)

❑ Client intake forms that include qualifying questions

❑ Programming activity attendance

❑ Incidents Reports

❑ Employee Time Sheets

❑ Expense Reports

❑ All Financial Transactions

❑ W4 form

❑ W2 form

❑ 1099 form

❑ I9 Form

❑ 990 Tax Forms

Establishing a Legitimate organization

Articles of Incorporation*

The Articles of Incorporation (sometimes also referred to as the Certificate of Incorporation or the Charter) are the primary rules governing the management of a corporation, and are filed with a state or other regulatory agency.

An organization's Articles of Incorporation generally provide information such as:

- The name of the person organizing the corporation (the Incorporator).
- If a business, the number of shares the corporation is authorized to issue.
- The names of the corporation's initial Board of Directors (though this is optional in most cases).

The location of the corporation's "registered office" - the location at which legal papers can be served to the corporation if necessary. Some states further require the designation of a Registered Agent: a person to whom such papers could be delivered.

Articles of Incorporation vary widely from corporation to corporation, and from jurisdiction to jurisdiction, but generally do not go into great detail about a corporation's operations, which are spelled out in more detail in a company's By-Laws.

Bylaws*

In a business situation, bylaws are drafted by a corporation's founders or directors under the authority of its Charter or Articles of Incorporation. Bylaws widely vary from organization to organization, but generally cover topics such as how directors are elected, how meetings of directors (and in the case of a business, shareholders) are conducted, and what officers the organization will have and a description of their duties.

Board of Directors*

A board of directors, also called board of trustees, board of governors, board of managers, or board of curators, is a group of individuals who govern the affairs of a corporation. The main duties of the board are to choose the chief executive officer and other officers to run the day-to-day operations of the corporation and to exercise high-level oversight. The board is run by the chairman of the board. Often the CEO serves concurrently as the chairman.

* Definitions taken from Answers.com

Answers.com delivers snapshot, multi-faceted definitions and explanations from credible, attributable reference sources on over one million topics in our database.

TAX EXEMPT STATUS**

Tax-exemption is an acknowledgment that the organization performs an activity that relieves some burden that would otherwise fall to federal, state, or local government. The government, in fact, provides an indirect subsidy to nonprofits and receives a direct benefit in return. Nonprofits also benefit the society as a whole when they provide valuable services. The viability of some of these services would be threatened if they were subject to taxes. Tax-exemption is afforded to churches as a safeguard to preserve separation of church and state by preventing governments from using taxation to favor one religion over another.

Almost all nonprofits are exempt from state and local property taxes; federal, state, and local income taxes; and state and local sales taxes. They are, however, required to pay taxes on income derived from activities that are unrelated to their mission. Nonprofits are not exempt from withholding payroll taxes for employees.

501 (c) (3) Determination Letter**

A determination letter is the most important legal document your organization possesses. The IRS sends you this letter after you have successfully applied for the recognition of your organization's tax-exempt status. In this document the IRS indicates under which section of the Internal Revenue Code your organization is qualified.

For instance, if you file Form 1023, you expect to be recognized as a 501(c)(3) tax-exempt organization. In order not to have your status revoked, your organization must continue operating according to the manner you described in your application.

The determination letter is the only official document and proof that your organization is recognized as a tax-exempt organization. Keep it in a safe place.

**Descriptions taken from www.BoardSource.org

BoardSource.org is dedicated to increasing the effectiveness of nonprofit organizations by strengthening their boards of directors.

ABILITY TO ACCOUNT FOR BOARD MEETING MINUTES

The Board of Directors consists of a Chairperson, Secretary, Treasurer and other members that may or may not be officers. The Chairperson is responsible for setting the meeting agenda and also for facilitating the meeting. The primary discussion topics and decisions regarding the topics are to be recorded in a book that can be referenced at a later date. Because the board can be bound to legal actions that may be taken towards the organization, policy issues that have been set in place need to be carefully documented. The wording needs to be considered and perhaps even reviewed by an attorney.

All Board minutes should indicate a date as well as the beginning time and ending time. The recorded minutes need to also include the names and affiliations of those in attendance. Some grant requirements insist that the grantee furnish a copy of the most recent board minutes. Many grant making entities use the board minutes to help discern the type of relationship and involvement that is practiced between the board and the rest of the organization.

Grants that involve servicing a specific population will require that the grantee demonstrate how an intentional effort is made to gain access to eligible participants. They need to provide evidence of an intentional and well-orchestrated outreach to ensure enrollment of the desired population.

To account for recruitment activities, an organization could document the names and contacts of the places where flyers were placed and distributed. The receipt for printing can serve as evidence for the amount of flyers purchased. Each activity that is documented should also include dates that they took place.

A Recruitment plan for a given project should also include samples of any press releases and flyer designs. It is a good idea to roster the types of responses that are generated from recruitment activities and to indicate the sources that produced responses as well as the efforts that were unfruitful. This information will also help to determine which recruiting methods will be most effective in the future. Remember to consider methods to identify the difference between the applicants that are eligible to receive your service as opposed to the ones who do not qualify.

Using the Table below list some recruiting activities on the left and then on the right indicate how you can give an accounting for how you carried out the activities listed.

Complete the exercise according to the example.

Recruiting Activities	Method of Accounting for Recruiting Activities
Ex. Use a Public Relations Specialist to identify market plan	➢ Submit a Copy of the help wanted ad ➢ Attach Resume and job application

Many service related grants require a set number of participants in order to show compliance with the grant contract. The grantors realize that there will be a certain level of attrition or a falling off from the number that may enroll. Grantees need to demonstrate their awareness that you will not complete the project with the same number of participants that first enrolled. At the same time grantees must provide evidence that they made an effort to recruit a larger number than the required quota.

When attempting to get initial enrollees, a sign-in sheet submitted at an event or at the designated offices will provide evidence of the outreach efforts. The sign-in sheet should include: Name, Address and phone number so that the enrollee can be checked. More personal information such as social security numbers, credit card numbers, etc. should not be required in a general sign-up sheet where other attendees can see that information.

Some grant projects may require employees and even volunteers to prove that they possess some form of picture ID and or a birth certificate, etc.

DISCUSSION

What are some of the ways that an organization can account for having enrolled a client?

_____
_____
_____
_____
_____
_____
_____
_____
_____
_____
_____

If your grant proposal gets selected to fund, it will be because you were able to persuade the potential funder that you can accommodate a need. In most cases the funder will be interested in helping you to address a specific population such as homeless children, HIV/AIDs victims, foster parents or perhaps welfare recipients. At the same time, when you announce that you r services are available, you will receive requests from people who do not fit the criteria for obtaining your service.

You will need some method to identify the difference between the applicants that can receive your service as opposed to the ones who do not qualify. For example, if you were being funded to have an after school program for blind teens, how would you account for those who would be considered eligible for service. How would you account for what made another applicant ineligible?

In the *Eligibility Intake Form Practice Table* on the next page, provide a qualifying category that would indicate if the applicant is eligible and a qualifying question that would help determine the types of services that might be given.

ELIGIBILITY INTAKE FORM PRACTICE TABLE

Type of Applicant	Qualifying Category	Qualifying Question/ Rationale
Ex. Disabled Veteran	Diagnosed Disability	When were you last treated for your disability? **Rationale**: This answer will indicate the length of disability as well as qualify if a disability exists.
At Risk Youth		
Substance Abusers		
Unwed mothers		

ABILITY TO ACCOUNT FOR BUDGETED EXPENDITURES

Fiscal Management is a very big issue when it comes to qualifying for funding from grants. Whoever is responsible for giving the go ahead to fund a particular project is in effect endorsing that entity as a good risk. This person is trusting that the grantee will manage the granted funds in such a way that will demonstrate a good investment and wise choice. On the other hand, a grantee that does a poor job with handling funds makes everyone involved look bad. Depending upon the degree of mismanagement someone could even lose employment. Reputations could also be damaged.

Largely due to the degree of risk involved, grantors are requiring grantees to *demonstrate* a system of accounting for *all* expenditures made with a grant funds. This is a reason that many non-profits are choosing to operate under the fiscal administrative umbrella of a more established organization. It is a practical and beneficial choice for a fledgling organization that desires to maintain the highest integrity regarding corporate financial management. It may indeed be the decision that helps to elevate smaller non-profits into reputable and sought out organization.

Some of the services that such a fiscal management organization may provide include:

- The receipting, accounting, and deposit of all donations.

- The disbursement of funds in accordance with approved purposes.

- Posting and bookkeeping of all transactions.

- Confirmations and reporting of all transactions to the founder.

- Preparation and filing of all federal, state, and local reports.

Since these fiscal management entities perform the administration work for your Foundation, non-profits are free to focus on delivering their charitable services and help those people who really need it. My newly formed non-profit received our first government funding using the National Heritage Foundation as a fiscal manager.

In addition to the crucial services that they provided, they also maintained a four star fiscal rating with the Charity Navigator.

For many start up organizations, government funds may be available to help finance legitimate initiatives to improve the community. Government grants provide the opportunity for people who have a stake in improving our nation to gain the resources needed to make a difference. At the same time the reporting and accountability requirements are quite rigid.

The rigidity of accounting for government funds is what helped us to demonstrate our ability to handle more donations from less restrictive donors. The National Heritage Foundation's fiscal integrity also helped us to qualify for resources that were generally reserved for larger and more established organizations than our new start up.

To get an idea of the type of account-ability required with government funds examine the following excerpt from a Request for Proposal (RFP) for an employment grant that was issued by the Department of Labor. *Highlight or underline the sections that you do not understand or that cause some concern.*

A. Budget Forms and Narrative Information

Each applicant must submit a cost proposal containing a completed Standard Form 424, ``Application for Federal Assistance;" a Standard Form 424A (Budget Information Form); and a detailed cost breakout for each column and line item from Section B of the Standard Form 424A.

In addition to these forms, the applicant must submit a ``detailed cost break out" that provides specific information on each of the expenditures listed under Section B of the Standard Form 424A, including both Federal and non-Federal funds. Each expenditure will fall under one of the three major cost categories: Administrative; Enrollee Wages and Fringe Benefits; or Other Participant Costs.

Explanations of these categories can be found earlier in these documents and in the SCSEP regulations at 20 CFR 641.404.

B. Fiscal and Performance Reporting Requirements

Applicants must have current computer technology and ensure that their organizations have the capability to link to the Internet.

Reporting must be done through the Internet.

In accordance with 29 CFR 97.40 or 29 CFR 95.51, each grantee must submit a Senior Community Service Employment Program Quarterly Progress Report (QPR). This report must be prepared to coincide with the ending dates for Federal fiscal year quarters and must be submitted to the Department no later than 30 days after the end of the quarterly reporting period. If the grant period ends on a date other than the last day of a federal fiscal year quarter, the last quarterly report covering the entire grant period must be submitted no later than 30 days after the ending date. The Department will provide instructions for the preparation of this report.

In accordance with 29 CFR 97.41 or 29 CFR 95.52, the following financial reporting requirements apply to title V grants:
--An SF-269, Financial Status Report (FSR), must be submitted to the Department within 30 days after the ending of each quarter of the program year.
-- A final FSR must be submitted within 45 days after the end of the grant.
- All FSRs must be prepared on an accrual basis. Charges incurred by a recipient during a given period requiring the provision of funds for: (1) goods and other tangible property received; (2) services performed by employees, contractors, subrecipients, and other payees; and (3) other amounts becoming owed under programs for which no current services or performance is required. [3]

---

[3] http://grants.gov/help/glossary.jsp

Use the table below to plan ways to account for some of the typical expenditures that may be addressed in a grant award. Write in some ideas about the way you would document or track the various types of expenditures that are listed on the left.

Budgeted Expense	TOTAL Expense $	Methods of Accounting & Tracking (Types of Documentation, etc)
Ex. Personnel	$ 175, 000	*Payroll reports, sign in sheets*
Personnel		
Fringe Benefits		
Operating/Technical		
Professional and Technical Services		
Materials and Supplies		
Equipment		
Travel		
Other (*explain*)		
TOTAL		

Budgets require budget narratives that offer detail about each expense. For example a staff person that is being compensated should also include 1) a brief summary about that person's responsibility and 2) the amount of time being contributed to the project.

Use the form below to practice developing a Project Budget Summary.

Budgeted Item	Description	Expense
Personnel		
EX. Executive Director	Oversee organizational operations (25% of total time- salary $100,000)	$25,000.00
Fringe Benefits		
Operating/Technical		
Professional and Technical Services		
Materials and Supplies		
Equipment		
Travel		
Other (explain)		
TOTAL		

A REASON WHY YOUR TAX EXEMPT STATUS IS NOT ENOUGH TO GET A GRANT

As a grant reviewer, I learned that many times having a 501 (c) (3) tax exempt status is not enough to receive certain grant dollars. The tax exempt status simply means that you are able to conduct business as a non-profit entity. There is no limit with regards to the number of staff you must hire. You also have a great deal of flexibility with deciding upon the services that you want to provide.

But what uninformed organizations do not know is that many of them are being turned down for grants because of the size of their budgets. The reasoning is that since you have not handled large sums of money already, you cannot be trusted to effectively manage a sizable grant award.

We were able to receive large amounts of grant dollars because we came under the umbrella of a management organization that specializes in helping organizations to get their foot in the door. Organizations like this can help start ups to focus on their service development without having to be concerned with the fiscal management of their program.

A good management organization will handle the incoming funds as well as keep track of all transactions and related reporting. Our even files the 990 tax form on our behalf. Their books are the ones that get audited on behalf of our program. I just have to address my own personal tax concerns.

Using a management organization as an umbrella worked so well for me that I learned how to do this for others. In fact, I helped a brand new (two years young) organization to receive over $300,000 dollars in federal grant dollars without having their own tax exempt status. This is significant because there is a special government audit that organizations experience if they receive over $300,000. The government requires that you contract an independent auditor to account for your expenditures. Our organization has always passed our audits with flying colors.

It is encouraging to meet well meaning individuals who want to do something to make a difference in the world. I encounter large numbers of people who express an interest in starting a non-profit organization in order to get tax exempt donations. However the high cost of filing fee (now $750) seems a bit much for start ups.

Many are also discouraged by the intimidating form that must accompany the fee. However, there is a way to get your foot in the door without going through this process. You can form your start up project and use a fiscal agent to receive donations.

HOW TO GET NON-PROFIT DONATIONS WITHOUT HAVING YOUR OWN 501 (C) (3) TAX EXEMPT STATUS

There are some basic steps that you should take in order to prepare to get a fiscal agent or engage an adoption organization offering monitoring and more involved support.

- Decide that you are going to specialize in a particular area of need such as homelessness, illiteracy, etc.

- Determine what type of people you will be serving, which is called your *target population*. For example you may decide to serve *at risk homeless youth* between the ages of 7 and 13.

- Identify the primary target location that you will be serving. It is generally best to serve an area that you can demonstrate as having a great need. This area may be an urban or rural community. But be specific about the geographic location using descriptions such as (for example) "the inner city community of Lawndale in Chicago, Illinois."

- Decide what service(s) you are going to offer, how you will carry it out and how much it will cost per person to provide the service.

- Find a location where your service(s) can be provided. You may provide this service at a location that is already established such as a school, library, community center, church, etc. Make sure that you get a written agreement that you may use this facility for a set period of time. This agreement should include a an exact description of the area promised (such as square footage, use of electricity, water, parking, etc.) with the address of the facility, as well a signature from someone *authorized* to give such permission.

• Neatly document the detailed plans for your project so that you and others will know what you are doing.

• Contact an organization to ask them to serve as your fiscal agent to offer you the tax exempt status needed for receiving donations. (See the Resource below for a national option). Any organization with a 501 (c)(3) tax exempt status in good standing may serve as your fiscal agent. The fiscal agent will also be responsible for completing the tax reporting to reflect what you received and paid. You will only be responsible for reporting your personal income received as wages. Donors simply need a means of writing off their donations in order to have tax breaks.

A fiscal agent will generally charge anywhere from 3.85% to 10% of your income in order to manage (receive and disburse) your funds.

Make sure that the fiscal agent that you choose files 990 tax returns. Ask to see a copy of the most recent return. If the organization has not received the amount of money that you are planning to get, find another organization.

Many non-profits are using organizations such as Congressional District Programs as a management organization because they go far beyond the services of a fiscal agent. The website is www.cdprograms.org.

Technical-ability is having and demonstrating the ability to apply technology in order to maximize productivity and efficiency. It takes into consideration the computer systems, applications and resources that are used to maximize administrative and programmatic efficiency. Technical-ability also includes having the ability to engage the technical communication, practices and policies that govern an area of interest..

The term *Technical Assistance* (TA) is a common term that non-profits often hear especially when they are grant recipients. This term applies to offering help that is specific to how they should properly function or operate. It assists with the technicalities or procedures regarding whatever is being considered. Therefore someone who is offering technical assistance regarding a youth development program will be familiar with the *best practices,* methods of operation and *policies* concerning those who work with youth.

When technical assistance is offered regarding grant proposal preparation, it includes information about the types of responses that are acceptable from the applicant. It also addresses the guidelines for *how* the grant proposal should be submitted along with eligibility, timelines, etc. Technical assistance for grant proposals will *not* assist with advising the actual individual responses to grant applications.

Non-profits and human services that apply the R.A.T.E.S. Principle of *Technical-ability* will actively pursue opportunities to receive technical assistance to learn more about their area of interest. They will also seek to learn about and apply enhancements in technology that will improve program delivery s well as administration.

TECHNOLOGY: BENEFITS AND CHALLENGES IN GRANT PROPOSALS

An obstacle that continues to prevent grass roots organizations from harnessing the efficiency of technology and office automation is the "digital divide." For example, if an organization does not have access to a computer system and a word processor, that organization will not produce documents and letters as efficiently as other organizations that do have that capability. Many grass roots organizations simply lack the time and resources to gain the appropriate knowledge that would help them to develop a workable technology strategy.

If organizations maintain a firm grasp of the basics, then they can take advantage of the services of a consultant that would help them to design the most cost effective and efficient solutions.   When or if organizations realize the need to upgrade or obtain an even more efficient application or system, they need to first understand the capabilities of what is already present.

RESEARCH AND EXPLAIN ANY UNUSUAL METHODS OR INNOVATIONS

In my grant proposals, the sections where I mentioned how our organization uses technology generally gave me high scores. I would include our using Quickbooks Pro® to manage our financial activities and reporting. I would also describe how we used Microsoft® Access database to log our activities and other information.

Smaller non-profits will do well to find innovative methods for using technology in administration and communication in the absence of state of the art resources. However when expressing these practices in a grant proposal, they should first research the appropriate wording or comparable description that is commonly understood. Grant proposal preparers would really benefit by first researching the acceptable technology standards for any activities that they plan to include. Even though their applications are working and they are seeing results, if the rest of the world may not accept this as the norm. Therefore, it may be necessary to go through a method of proving that their uses of technology are effective.

Or if the project is able to save time and money because of an innovation that is being used, it simply needs to be sufficiently explained. I made the mistake of not explaining an innovative method for using technology.   Even though my application of this technology was not commonly accepted, I had expected the reviewers to simply take my word that we could do it. Since the reviewers do not know you, they have to be convinced that you are stating the truth and giving them facts. You have to somehow let them get to know and believe you.

A growing number of non-profit organizations are feeling compelled to cut staff while trying to maintain a quality of productivity that will allow them to remain viable. An effective way of maximizing the efficiency of a small staff is through the use of technology.   Grass roots organizations are also finding that the reporting demands by funders can greatly hinder their ability to carry out the programming for their projects. Automating the data entry can provide a significant time saver.

THE ABILITY TO APPLY TECHNOLOGY BASED COMMUNICATION

Those organizations that seek to practice *Technical-ability* should commit to demonstrating the ability to use technology-based skills that include: communication, recording, documentation and reporting. Applications that maximize efficiency in technology communications include the following:

Image: Web site, brochures, cards, newsletters, Presentations

Correspondence: Notebook computer; Word processing, Laser quality printer; Email, Scheduling Program (Lotus Organizer, ACT, MS Outlook)

Communication: Answering Service; Voice mail with a paging attendant; Cell Phone

Organization: Spreadsheets Databases, Daily Planner; Project manager, Accounting Software

Today's' technology arena offers a wide variety of solutions to enhance an organization's ability to function at maximum capacity. For example, documents are prepared on a word processor. Newsletters are no longer prepared by just using a Desktop publishing application. Newsletters may be developed through web based applications and even distributed through electronic email.

Nonprofit organizations should conduct self assessments to help determine their technology needs. Each organization must be assessed according to their organizational makeup as well as their goals and objectives. Effective technology assessments will take into account the present status along with future projections.

TechAtlas is an online tool that provides a free technology assessment tool. It is a very useful on-line tool that provides: Articles, Resources, and Worksheets, to help you learn more about what technical terms mean, such as RAM, Operating Systems, and Hard Drives, networks and more. The TechAtlas Planning Center and TechSurveyor Asset

Management Center both include a glossary of Technology Terms, nonprofit-friendly explanations of technology concepts, and links to resources to learn more. Sometimes, you can even use a worksheet to take your new information and make it work for your organization. Example resource topics include: Staffing for Technology, Budgeting for On-Going Technology Costs and Fundraising for New Technology.

The website address is www.Techatlas.org.

Many times organizations have purchased computer-based solutions when they already had what was needed from the earlier purchase. They simply did not understand the capabilities of what they had. It is difficult to ask the appropriate questions without first having a basic understanding office technology.

When preparing a budget to purchase or upgrade a system it is good to understand the basic terms that are used in computer technology. Assess your familiarity with basic computer terms by tapping into the online tools.

THE ABILITY TO APPLY TECHNOLOGY BASED REPORTING

A database allows for collecting information that can be manipulated and summarized to produce specific types of reports. It also allows for gathering certain types of information to obtain statistical information.

A database is a collection of information that's related to a particular subject or purpose, such as tracking customer orders or maintaining a music collection. If your database isn't stored on a computer, or only parts of it are, you may be tracking information from a variety of sources that you're having to coordinate and organize yourself.*

The reporting demands have been notorious for causing many small grass roots organizations to want to throw in the towel. The first round of reporting can be the most overwhelming. However a planned information input and output system can make reporting much less cumbersome.

For example if your project requires you to provide information concerning the number of participants according to gender, you would need an efficient method of separating your information. Your report will need to reflect the number of males as well as the number of females. It may not be very practical or efficient to separate the documents with this information into separate piles of male and female applicants and to then count them.

However, if you had this information in a database, a simple report could quickly and accurately produce the totals that are required.

The internet is a widely used database that provides connectivity and access to a vast universe of services, products and information. Organizations that have internet capabilities will be able to develop at a much better pace than those who do not have internet access. The options provided through the internet can greatly enhance the process of planning for technological enhancements.

Technology planning is being practiced by nonprofit organizations so that they can become more productive and sustaining. According to an on-line technology assistance organization called TechSoup, "a technology plan is the single most important ingredient to effectively using technology in your organization. The technology planning process will help minimize technology-related crises, use staff time efficiently, and avoid wasting money on equipment. Create a plan to help you think through your priorities in order to use technology in a way that directly furthers your mission."

TechSoup is one of the nation's oldest and largest nonprofit technology assistance agencies. Their services are open to all qualified 501c3 nonprofit organizations. The TechSoup website is powered by CompuMentor. TechSoup.org offers nonprofits a one-stop resource for technology needs by providing free information, resources, and support. In addition to online information and resources, they offer a product philanthropy service called TechSoup Stock. Nonprofits can access donated and discounted technology products, generously provided by corporate and nonprofit technology partners.

TechSoup provides instructional articles and worksheets for nonprofit staff members who utilize information technologies, as well as technology planning information for executives and other decision makers. Their introductory articles and message board support are aimed at those who do not have much experience using technology, however they also provide more advanced information.

The Techsoup website address is: www.Techsoup.org.

Consider the importance of using technology to improve service delivery and administration.

Begin Assessing your Organization's Ability to Apply Technology using the following:

Technical Ability Item	Good	OK	Don't Have
Hardware System			
Computer systems (Monitors, CPU's, keyboards, mouse(s), Operating Systems			
Printer(s)			
Copier(s) /Scanner(s)			
Fax Machine(s)			
Modem			
Notebook or Laptop Computer			
Tape backup unit, zip drive			
Un-interruptible Power Supply (UPS)			
Software System			
Word Processor /Desktop Publisher			
Spreadsheet Application			
Database			
Accounting Software			
Internet Access			
Daily Planner/Organizer			
Communication			
Answering Service/ Voice Mail			
Cell Phone			
Fax number			
Email			
Image			
Business cards			
Newsletters			
Web Site			

EVALUATION-ABILITY

Evaluation-ability is having and demonstrating the ability to engage an independent and unbiased evaluator who will assess the strengths and challenges of your organization and related projects. The results of the evaluations will help develop strategies for ongoing improvements.

Evaluation is about documenting results that prove what was accomplished and to what extent a project was successful. When Jesus was asked if he was the one, by John's disciples, he offered proof according to what he accomplished as testimony that he was in fact the One that was to come.

Each project should have an element of salvation in order to be viable. Participants must have the evidence that they are being saved from something that would otherwise cause them suffering. An evaluation will uncover of salvation actually occurred and also offer reasons about the degree of success or failure.

Each project or program needs to be evaluated with methods that will provide objective assessments. The results of these assessments can help to determine the strengths and weaknesses of a project or even the overall program. An organization needs to think in terms of what systems are in place to assess organizational efficiency.

There is an excellent report commissioned by the W.K. Kellog Foundation on the results of a 2002 grantmaker's conference. The conference by Grantmakers for Effective Organizations, was in partnership with Forum of Regional Associations of Grantmakers, Grantmakers Evaluation Network. The report includes a section titled, "Measure for Measure: Evaluating Grantmaker Effectiveness. It describes how grantmakers should view their grantees with regards to the evaluation process. In the article the author begins with the following statement, "Grantmakers across the country regularly challenge their grantees to think in new ways about their own effectiveness and how to measure it."

WHAT EXACTLY IS A PROJECT EVALUATION?

A project evaluation includes: 1) getting information about the purpose of a project 2) The methods of carrying out the project 3) Assessing the factors that contributed to the results of the project 4) Making recommendations regarding the project. An evaluation is made when information and data are assembled about the project in order to assess any related actions that need to be taken. The information supplied from an evaluation can also help to determine the degree of success as well as how to address barriers to success of a project.

EVALUATION PROCESS

Your evaluation plan should be simple, focused, and appropriate to the specific goals of your project. Only collect data that is directly related to project activities. Your plan should include:

- Develop specific evaluation questions (questions about how the project will be carried out and the measurable outcomes)

- Specific indicators and measures that will be used to evaluate project success

- Specific data collection methods that will be used

- The timeline for evaluation data collection

- Describe how evaluation findings will be used to improve the project.

MAJOR EVALUATION CONCEPTS

Evaluations can be simple or very complex. They can include information that will effect specific areas of a project or program. When dealing with social services or other projects that involve treating or responding to the needs of clients, evaluations tend to become more complex. For example according to a report by Rob Orwin, Ph.D.

entitled "Battelle Centers for Public Health Research and Evaluation", evaluations should include three major concepts, which are as follows:

Process evaluation—evaluation activities related to an assessment of a treatment

provider's operations; increasingly becoming synonymous with an assessment of the degree of conformity to the design (also generically termed: implementation evaluation)

Impact or outcomes evaluation—evaluation of whether and to what extent a treatment approach or bundle of services causes changes in the desired direction among the target population

Cost analysis—the identification and analysis of all resources needed for a treatment provider's operations; studies of the relationship between treatment costs and treatment outcomes, with both costs and outcomes expressed in monetary terms (Rossi et al., 1993)[4].

There is an excellent report commissioned by the W.K. Kellogg Foundation on the results of a 2002 grantmaker's conference. The conference by Grantmakers for Effective Organizations, was in partnership with Forum of Regional Associations of Grantmakers, Grantmakers Evaluation Network. The report includes a section titled, "Measure for Measure: Evaluating Grantmaker Effectiveness. It describes how grantmakers should view their grantees with regards to the evaluation process. In the article the author begins with the following statement, "Grantmakers across the country regularly challenge their grantees to think in new ways about their own effectiveness and how to measure it."

Organizations may be apprehensive about evaluators because they represent a determining factor in regards to the type of funding as well as the amount that may be invested. For example, an evaluator may determine that an organization simply does not have the capacity to carry out the program for which it is requesting funds. This

---

[4] This document was produced by the Center for Substance Abuse Treatment, Department of Health and Human Services, Caliber/NEDTAC Contract No. 270-94-0001 and is being made available through Caliber/NEDS Contract No. 270-97-7016. 1999.

assessment is generally based upon answers to questions and observations. Some organizations have expressed concern in the questions that are being presented not being appropriate to assess how organizations are doing what they do.

Evaluations are typically based upon a pool of past experiences. Therefore if a "well run" youth program typically employs a project manager, secretary and bookkeeper and a certified youth social worker then other programs that lack in any of these areas may be considered to be running over capacity. I remember applying for a grant and stating that we would produce a multi-media video program in two weeks and receiving low points because the reader thought that it was not nearly enough time to complete such a project.

The proposal was based upon our experience and the formula for the format that we were using. However, as the grantee, we needed to convince the grantor that we had mastered a technology that they did not know existed.

Likewise an evaluator may prepare questions about how something will take place with a preconception about how it *could* happen. We were once asked to list everything that our organization does by a program evaluator. The evaluator was immediately convinced that we do too much because of the list and because of our own limited *paid* staff. We were never asked who was responsible for each of the projects. The answers to that question would have shed some light on things.

For example, for the feeding program, we had women who would come to prepare the meals. To give out packaged food, we had people in the neighborhood that would bag the goods and help with distribution.

We began taking the children in our youth program to other organizations that provided services we did not offer, while helping them with skills that they needed to develop. An independent evaluation uncovered that our true expertise was in the ability to enlist services and support *from* and *for* other grass roots organizations. We were fortunate to have a funder that invited us to partner in the evaluation process.

In his book, "An Insider's Guide to Grantmaking[5]" Joel J. Orosz illustrates 4 principles of best practices regarding evaluations. These principles are as follows:

PRINCIPLE 1: Good project evaluation is good grant management, and good grant management is good program evaluation.

The purpose of the evaluator should be to help the grant recipient become more effective and more efficient and not as a tool for disqualification. Mr. Orosz expresses that the evaluator should be viewed as part of the management team for the project and concerned with achieving "*the highest standards of project management.*"

PRINCIPLE 2: Project evaluation should be owned primarily be the applicant and designed primarily for the applicant's use.

In many cases the evaluation for a project is commissioned by and then owned by a grantor or funder. Because of this, the grantee is left with the anxiety of wondering if the results of an evaluation will be used in some report to demonstrate the inadequacies of a project. However, the evaluation results can be used by the grant recipients to help their staff address some of the areas of weakness as well as build upon the strengths.

PRINCIPLE 3: The most important decisions about evaluation need to be made by the stakeholders in the project.

Anyone who does not have something to gain or lose from the results of the project will not view the evaluation process or information appropriately. According to Orosz, leaving stake holders (grantees) out of the decisions resulting from the evaluation "*all but guarantees that stakeholders will get an evaluation plan that does not fit their needs.*"

PRINCIPLE 4: The stakeholders need to identify the important questions they wish the evaluation to address.

---

[5] Joel J. Orosz; *The Insider's Guide to Grantmaking*. Jossey-Bass, San Francisco: A Wiley Company, 2000. pp86-87

The grantee is the one who will be most affected by the results of the evaluation. The grantee can make the best of the evaluation process by first considering the questions that need to be asked in order to insure the success, continuation and growth of the project. Orosz states that the answers to the specific questions developed by the stake holders will also help determine who the evaluator should be and how much the evaluation might cost.

The ability to develop appropriate questions that will help in project or program assessment will determine an organization's ability to ability to evaluate the program or project.

The best place to start in developing questions for an evaluation is to first have a clear understanding of what the project is about. The goals and objectives need to be concise and determined with the consideration of how the outcomes can possibly be measured.

GOALS AND OBJECTIVES

GOALS – Describe what major accomplishment(s) will be achieved by meeting the need(s) described in the Problem Statement and/ or Needs Assessment. *There should only be 1 to 2 Goals per proposal.

OBJECTIVES – Describe the outcomes that must be accomplished in order to meet the needs that are related to the stated Goal(s).

*There will be a detailed work plan or method to account for and achieve each objective.

In any organization, there needs to be clearly stated goals and objectives. These goals and objectives will help determine the actions needed to realize success. Without clearly defined and mutually understood goals, an organization may find itself grossly unproductive.

The organization may well be accomplishing many things and doing great works. However, if these accomplishments are not in line with the stated goals and objectives, then the organization becomes disjointed and unorganized.

A disjointed organization suffers from a staff that has difficulty staying focused. An unfocused staff deprives an organization of having a firm foundation that is needed to sustain and even expand.

Completing a work plan from goals and objectives that can be evaluated

Example

GOAL: Provide construction related job training program for youth.

Example

OBJECTIVE 1: 50 youth will be recruited to receive construction related job training.

OBJECTIVE 2: 75% of enrolled youth will complete attend a 5 –day orientation.

OBJECTIVE 3: 50% of youth completing our program will obtain employment within 120 days after completion.

Simple Work Plan Sample:

Objective 1-Y*outh will be recruited to receive construction related job training.*

Task(s)	Time Frame	Responsible Position
Develop Informational Flyers promoting Job Training	First month after grant award	Administrative Assistant
Outreach to Community Stakeholders to Promote Job Training	Ongoing	Program Director
Develop Sign In Sheets and Informational Material	First month	Program Director / Administrative Assistant

Having the ability to document Goals, Objectives and Activities will assist with the development of effective Evaluation Plans.

Think about a primary Goal that you would like to achieve and some measurable Objectives needed to reach that goal.

Use the following table to practice developing Goals and Objectives.

GOALS AND OBJECTIVES WORK TABLE

GOAL THAT IS ADDRESSED	OBJECTIVES (Steps taken to meet the stated Goal)
Goal # 1	Objective #1
	Objective # 2
	Objective # 3

Sustain-ability is having and demonstrating the ability to sustain by continuing to provide support and development for your organization. Sustain-ability is accomplished through diverse and effective resource and revenue development activities.

Sustainability efforts provide the ability to continue the program beyond the grant amount that is awarded by a funder or donors. Organizations should carefully consider alternatives to funding and even work performance with a reduced staff. There is no way of knowing for certain that funds that have even been promised will absolutely become available when scheduled. This is especially true with government funds.

However even private and corporate donors need to know that an organization is looking to them for limited support and is not solely dependent upon their contributions for existence. Many donors may reason that an organization would plan on being able to sustain in the event that the donor could no longer continue to provide financial assistance. Funders want to know that they are not the only source of funds that is being used by an organization. They want to know that the organization has the support of the community as well as other donors.

In every Request for Proposal (RFP) that our organization has responded to, we have been asked about our plans to *sustain*. There is generally a point system that helps to determine if an applicant ranks high enough to receive the grant award. The ability to sustain a project is generally a high ranking category.

Financial assistance can be halted for a number of reasons. For example a donor may die suddenly without having made provisions for a project or program that may have even been favored. However the organization has to deal with the reality that the funds simply stopped coming after the donor is deceased.

Some other unfortunate instances that may occur include an economic influence that reduces the amount of giving overall. Often when the economy becomes questionable or unstable, philanthropists make significant reductions in their giving.

A secret to sustaining is partnering with other organizations that will add your proposal contents to theirs. If you can make their proposals more compelling with what you bring to the table, they will want to keep collaborating with you.

You can also get funded through *Partnership Agreements* where you provide services for organizations that have been issued grant awards. There are a number of resources available in order to find funded organizations that might need the services that you offer. The Foundation Center website has a great tool for searching for organizations that have submitted a 990 tax report and are located in *your* region. (www.foundationcenter.org) Send the organizations a letter explaining your experience and that you would be willing to complete your portion of your proposal. Be prepared to have an *Executive Summary* that will provide a better idea about how you might fit in. (See page 113 for an overview of *Executive Summary*.)

Using this strategy allowed me to help raise millions of dollars for my students. I recognized through my own experience that collaborative projects are much more attractive for a number of reasons. One of the main reasons that collaborations are good investments is that each entity has its own connection and resources.

The leaders of other organizations are also social entrepreneurs. As social entrepreneurs they are accustomed to taking risks. They are not like employees who are simply interested in a paycheck. They are stakeholders who recognize that supporting your efforts will make it easier for them to gain their own success.

Even in a slow economy, grants for essential social, economic, health and institutional issues are still made available. Grants are funds awarded in response to a plan submitted as a grant proposal for addressing these or other issues

Gaining an understanding about the nature of a proposal really began with our receiving a letter stating that we were awarded the grant, but for less money than we requested. My husband and I were really concerned about this because we had calculated how much we thought it would cost to run this particular program. My husband, who had become the budget preparation expert, had already found ways to cut costs to a bare minimum.

We even requested less money than we thought was needed in an effort to be more competitive. That was a BIG MISTAKE. Organizations should always be realistic with requesting funds that will allow them to successfully meet the goals and objectives that they plan.

But through our protest regarding the reduction in the amount awarded, we learned another lesson that was perhaps one of the greatest lessons. This lesson is that since grant proposals are contracts, they are negotiable.

Therefore since the grant award amount was reduced, we could adjust the projected outcomes accordingly. In other words if we propose a budget of $100,000 to service 100 youth and we are only awarded a grant for $80,000, then we can adjust the projected service number to 80 youth (or less). I learned how to renegotiate the projected outcomes and submit a budget revision which really helped the organization that we were working for at the time. Before the contract revision, the organization would have surely fallen short of meeting their program requirements.

A grant proposal documents what the submitting organization plans to do about a problem. The same proposal also serves as the framework for a contract that binds the organization to complete the work that they propose.

BASICS FOR WRITING GRANT PROPOSALS

While there are certain basics of writing grant proposals, the categories of required information may vary according to the type and amount of funding being requested. For example, a grant proposal that is seeking to cover costs for a bus to transport homeless people will not need all of the same type of information as one seeking funds to operate an after school program.

Many times a grant proposal will be submitted in response to a Request for Proposal (or RFP) from a funding source. The content of the RFP will influence the content of the grant proposal.

Grant proposals that are organized in sections make it easier for donors to locate the information. Every section should reinforce whatever issue is being proposed for funding. All of the responses provided in each section should clearly relate to the primary issue presented in the grant proposal.

The following briefly describes the basic sections that should be included when writing grant proposals:

PROBLEM STATEMENT

A *Problem Statement* identifies something wrong that is in urgent need of a solution. Keep in mind that the types of problems identifying significant pain, suffering or hardship for others will have the greatest chance for getting funded. For example, consider the following: There has been a 20% increase in substance abuse related arrests among juveniles between ages 18 through 24. Statistics from the XYZ Global Youth Initiative indicates that a common trigger for substance abuse among juveniles in this age range is social isolation.

The problem statement in the example above plainly identifies something wrong. It also indicates who has the problem and how much the problem is making an impact. This problem statement also suggests a root cause for the problem.

Notice that it did not have to address the totality of the problem, but only an area that may be addressed in the grant proposal.

NEEDS STATEMENT

The needs statement describes a lack of resources required to solve a problem. For example, a portion of the needs statement could include: The social isolation that triggers the problem of substance abuse among juveniles between ages 18 through 24 reveals a need for developing socialization skills. There is a critical shortage of counselors who are able to teach socialization skills to this age group in our county.

There are distinct differences between problem statements and needs statements. However some RFPs may only have a heading for either one or the other. If this is the case, then it will be prudent to prepare the information for both the problem and the needs and include them under the one heading that is allowed. Even though there may not be a clear request to explain a problem or need, this information will certainly be expected in your grant proposal.

GOALS

A goal is a general statement about the intent to reduce or eliminate a problem. It summarizes the answer about what the plan is to make the problem go away. For example, the goal could be to prevent youth (ages 18-24) from going to jail for substance abuse related charges.

Be aware when writing grant proposals, that each goal will include a set of objectives. When offered a grant, you will be held accountable to meet the goals and objectives that your grant proposal documented. For this reason, I strongly recommend that your first attempts in writing grant proposals should not include more than three goals.

OBJECTIVES

The outcomes needed to help meet the goals make up the objectives. These steps must be measurable so that they can be later proven. Suppose a grant proposal is using the goal given in the example contained in this material. In that case an objective could be as follows: *To develop alternative sentencing options for 50 youth arrested for substance use related charges.* The number of youth in this example is what will be measured. Also notice that the objective clearly connects with the stated goal.

The steps given in objectives should indicate what will take place or happen. There will be a detailed work plan or method describing how and when the objectives will be completed.

Program objectives require specific activities that must be done. These activities must directly result in meeting the given objectives. For example if there is an objective to hold 5 workshops about time management, one of the activities could be to design flyers to promote the workshops.

PROGRAM ACTIVITIES

Activities that are not well planned are often not carried out with much success. Even an activity that appears as insignificant as preparing flyers may hinder the success of a project. If there is not enough thought about producing a flyer, the resulting appearance may be unattractive. An unattractive flyer will not draw people appropriately.

Also if the essential activity is not documented among the plans, then it may not be addressed at all. What would happen if only a few days before the workshops are to take place, someone realizes that the event has not even been adequately publicized? This happens much more than you might think.

IMPLEMENTATION

This section may be called different names such as "Methodology" or "Scope of Services", depending upon the type of grant or preferences of the grantor. However, the body of information is essentially the same when writing grant proposals. This section will illustrate a project design that describes a plan to meet the goals and objectives.

The implementation is the section of a grant proposal for describing what will be done and how the activities will be carried out. It will also determine the type of staffing and resources needed to make the proposed project successful. The implementation will illustrate a brief walk through of what clients or participants will actually experience when they participate in the project. The sequential activities outlined in this section should include a general timeline for when they are expected to take place or be completed.

ORGANIZATIONAL CAPACITY

After the plans to reduce or eliminate a problem have been effectively described in the implementation section, the grant proposal still needs to prove that the applicant has the ability to make it happen. This section should demonstrate that the applicant has a good idea of what it will take to run the project which includes adequate staffing and resources.

The capacity is the sufficiency of the staffing, resources etc. to make sure that the project produces favorable results. This section will also offer brief bios of the primary personnel that will be working on behalf of the organization requesting funding. Any past experience for providing related services should also be included here.

EVALUATION PLAN

Everyone who receives funds for their projects will be required to prove the extent their project was beneficial. The evaluation plan in a grant proposal will demonstrate "how" as well as "how much" things change for the better as a result of what was done. The evaluation plan also describes the type of information that will be collected and reported to assess the proposed effort or project.

The evaluation data will provide facts and figures about the effect on the goals, objectives and project implementation. An evaluation allows donors to have a measurable accounting of how impacting their contribution was. NOTE: I highly recommend that this portion of the grant proposal is completed with someone who understands evaluation concepts.

BUDGET

Many people make the mistake of using the same figures for the project budget and the organizational budget. A project budget is different from an organizational budget even though both must be considered in a grant proposal. For example, an organizational budget may include the cost for: rent, telephones, supplies and the Executive Director. On the other hand, a project budget should display only the portion of the rent, telephones, supplies and the Executive Director that is dedicated to the project.

The salary for the Executive Director is a common budgetary item where grant proposals are especially scrutinized.

In a project budget, The Executive Director should be compensated according to how much of his or her time is spent on the project. Therefore if the organization pays the Executive Director $65,000, the project budget may only allow for the percentage of time that the Executive Director will spend on the project. If this is 50% of the time, then the project budget should reflect 50% of the total (organizational) salary which is $32,5000.

BUDGET NARRATIVE

A grant proposal budget needs to be complete with calculations that show how each cost was determined. This detail is summarized in a budget narrative. Budget narratives are required to offer a brief explanation about why and how money is being spent. The justification for the expenses should reflect the stated goals, objectives and project implementation

ABSTRACT

An abstract is a summary of the project that generally includes the brief information regarding the problem, needs, overall plan, target population, cost and experience of the applicant. This synopsis is generally contained on one page and may also be used for press releases.

EXECUTIVE SUMMARY

An executive summary is a more expanded detail that may include a summary from every section in the proposal. The executive summary should be limited to between 2 and 4 pages. Both the abstract and executive summary is developed after a proposal is completed. However they are generally the first documentation that a reviewer will read.

When you are awarded a grant, the contents of your grant proposal will be used to develop the contract requirements for the money that you are given. With this in mind, your grant proposal should only include what you know you can accomplish with the amount that you are requesting.

Regardless of the grant source, your ability to receive and continue to acquire funding will rely upon your efforts to make your case in writing.

Banks oversee many of the 75,000 private foundations in the U.S. This is a number that's more than doubled in the last 12 plus years according to an article by U.S. Banker. Bank of America has 1,022 foundations for its high net worth clients, more than any other bank, according to the nonprofit Foundation Center in Washington, D.C.

"It's very common to see a bank as the contact entity for a private foundation," says Loren Renz, vice president for research at the Foundation Center. This is especially the case among "smaller" foundations, those with assets of less than $10 million, says Renz.

But there's plenty of room for growth. Although private foundations control about $200 billion — they gave away $11.3 billion in 2000 — the number of private foundations is tiny compared with the number of high net worth clients. Among the 700,000 families with $5 million or more in net assets — who last year gave $32 billion to charity.

Private foundations are required to donate 5% of their total assets each year and pay a 1% excise tax to the IRS on money earned in investments.

This means that as long as foundations exist there is always the possibility of obtaining funds from donors. Grass Roots Organizations need to learn how to publicize their mission and needs. However they also have to assure potential donors that their projects will be a sound and worthwhile investment.

Even though the U.S. economy has been hit hard with high unemployment, high foreclosure rates and other societal issues that pull on resources, there remains an effort by donors to continue giving. *The Foundation Center estimates that foundation assets rebounded slightly in 2009, rising 3.3 percent to $583.4 billion, and that giving will remain flat in 2010. As the economic recovery falters, the outlook beyond 2010 remains unclear, but there continues to be potential for modest positive growth in 2011 foundation giving.*[6]

---

[6] The Foundation Center, Foundation Yearbook, 2010. Foundation Yearbook is part of the Foundations Today Series of annual research reports on foundation growth and giving.

While having to develop methods of sustaining, we had to research and find out what other successful organizations were doing to raise funds. Our studies revealed that Nonprofit organizations have found the need to development programs committed to increase the available financial resources to support their mission and vision. They need to plan for identification, solicitation, procurement and management of public and private funding.

There needs to be someone assigned to cultivate an established relationship with potential community partners. This person may ask community partners to provide copies of all requests for proposals that may meet program guidelines and documents in-kind services to the program. He or she might also seek to solicit local business partners to sponsor special events, including purchasing the food and T-shirts for participants. This person can assemble a program advisory committee who will put a high priority on expanding community partnerships as quickly as possible. The more "ownership" the community and partners have, the more likely the program will continue.

The program advisory committee will be asked to conduct an inventory of all available support for the program. The funding sources include cash resources from community partners.

A number of organizations have used retreats to offer a comfortable setting for stakeholders, board members, etc. to unite in financial and resource development for an organization. Community leaders, residents, and the program staff can participate in the retreat. Among their objectives, they may plan to develop a long-term plan for the continuation of primary programs. One significant portion of the plan may include laying out a funding strategy that ensures the continuation of the program for at least five years. It is commonly suggested by strategic retreat facilitators that letters of support from the partners are drafted and attached to any agreement s. They stress that these signed agreements should be secured *before* the end of the retreat.

Before beginning a fundraising campaign it is important to plan a strategy that is achievable considering the resources of an organization. In many instances a collaborative fundraising program may be even more successful. When organizations work together they have a better chance of maximizing the investment. A greater investment can produce a greater return.

Part of the planning may include researching giving trends. Knowing the group of people that are more likely to contribute to your cause will help to target funding expenses. For example a recent study in giving practices revealed that the elderly appeared to be more generous than younger donors. It also revealed that both the probability and the amount of giving increases monotonically with age. The study stated that those age 65-74 are 24 percent more likely to make a gift than those aged 45-54.

Here are highlights of giving trends compiled by the Foundation Center:

KEY FINDINGS FROM THE FOUNDATION GIVING TRENDS REPORT

Funding for education grew fastest among major program areas. Giving for education increased 18.9 percent to $4.5 billion in 2001, surpassing other major subject areas and the 11.6 percent overall increase in grant dollars in the sample. Education also continued to account for the largest share of overall foundation support (26.8 percent). Among grants benefiting education was the largest grant ever recorded: the William and Flora Hewlett Foundation's $400 million award to Stanford University for unrestricted endowment support, as well as to support professorships, graduate fellowships, and undergraduate scholarships and programs.

Support for student aid reached record share. Giving to organizations for student aid grew 77.5 percent in 2001 to $1.9 billion. This raised the share of funding for scholarships, fellowships, and other forms of student aid from 7.1 percent to 11.3 percent of grant dollars-the highest share on record. Close to half of the dollars awarded for student aid funds supported graduate and postdoctoral fellowships, including the Ford Foundation's $275.5 million award to the International Fellowships Fund, while two-fifths supported scholarships for undergraduates.

Children and youth benefited from a record share of grant dollars. Foundations in the sample directed fewer than two out of five of their grant dollars ($6.2 billion) to named population groups in the 2001 sample. Among these grants, children and youth continued to account for the largest share of support-a record 17.9 percent of overall grant dollars, up from 16.6 percent in 2000. The economically disadvantaged retained the second largest share of grant dollars-12.1 percent, down from 16.4 percent in the prior year.

International support lost share, although actual giving was stable. Support for international giving-which includes grants to overseas recipients and funding for international programs in the U.S.-remained almost unchanged at $2.46 billion in 2001. As a share of overall foundation funding in the sample, international giving declined from a record 16.3 percent to 14.7 percent. Yet this share remained well above the 10 percent to 11 percent of grant dollars that targeted international purposes in the 1990s. Giving to overseas recipients decreased from $901.3 million to $770.7 million, while support for U.S.-based international programs increased from $1.5 to $1.7 billion. Among international grants was one of the year's largest award: the Bill & Melinda Gates Foundation's $100 million grant to the Global Fund to Fight AIDS, Tuberculosis, and Malaria for its Global Fund for AIDS and Health.

PREPARING FOR SOLICITATION

It can be especially difficult for organizations that find they have to learn skills for soliciting funds. If the Board of Directors is unfamiliar or unable to solicit funds than it becomes necessary for someone else in the organization to adapt these skills in order to keep the organization afloat. Directors of non-profit organizations find that they have to learn to become attractive to donors because the donors often give to organizations because they like the people as well as the cause.

Often the grass roots organizations appear to be at a disadvantage because they simply cannot afford to hire fundraisers and do not have the time to cultivate relationships. Hope grass roots organizations that have great programs will also began to see that it is well worth the investment to take the time to cultivate relationships with donors as well as even consider contracting fundraisers.

The Enterprise Foundation offers services to non-profit organizations including a working database that lists funders. Their resources include on-line internet training. One segment of their training addresses fund raising. In the preparation segment they provide really sound tips. The following is an example of their tips for preparing a solicitation:

There are three phases to preparing a solicitation:[7]

Target

Know what you need, and what you're asking for.

Do your homework! Research, and know as much as possible about your funder.

Be able to link your request to the funder's interests and priorities. If they want to know,
"What's in it for me," be prepared to tell them!

If possible, do a preliminary visit to establish a personal relationship and "test the waters."
get a sense about how they like your idea … are they receptive? Do they have suggestions about how to strengthen your proposal?

Logistics

If requested to do so, prepare a letter of inquiry.

Set up the appointment.

---

[7] The Enterprise Foundation 10227 Wincopin Circle, Suite 500, Columbia, MD 21044; WEBSITE: www.Enterprisefoundation.org.

The Enterprise also does a great job with summarizing the different types of support that is available. The following list is taken from The Enterprise Foundation on-line course:

Support for your organization will come in different forms and will meet different needs. It can often be pulled together under the auspices of a campaign with a goal, a set of strategies and a time frame. Some donors like to feel as though they are contributing to a larger goal and that their funds are being leveraged to attract others. Because of the shifting focus of donors, the growing interest in leveraging funds and the benefits of cultivating new relationships, nonprofits should look to raise different types of support, such as:

Capital grants are earmarked for principal projects to meet future service demands, such as purchase, construction or renovation of a physical facility, land acquisition or major equipment purchase.

Challenge (matching) grants: Restricted or unrestricted grants may be made in the form of a challenge to the organization to raise an equal or specified amount from other sources. The grant is contingent upon the matching funds being raised.

Endowments are grants providing for an organization's future security. Endowment funds are invested to provide annual income, usually as a percentage of income earned.

In-kind support: No cash is given with in-kind support. Organizations or individuals may be able to provide you with products or services that you need to do business. A graphic designer might donate time to design and produce your newsletter or organizational brochure; a local corporation might be able to provide a loaned executive to help you with a specific issue; or a local hardware store might donate paint or other building supplies. Be sure, however, that you want and can use the products they can provide. You do not want to have to warehouse 100 cans of paint if you cannot use them.

Program or project grants support a specific program, usually with measurable outcomes.

Restricted grants: Restricted funds are limited to specific purposes as outlined in the proposal or otherwise specified by the donor.

Seed money is for experimental, innovative or start-up projects (pilot or demonstration programs). Depending on initial outcomes, funding may be renewable. Seed funding is attractive; it enables an organization to "test the waters" and prove its viability in order to attract or leverage funding from other sources.

Unrestricted grants: The funds can be used for any purpose. They are often the hardest to get because donors often want their money spent on a specific project. But, unrestricted giving provides the most flexibility on how to use the funds.

PLANNING YOUR FUNDRAISING PROGRAM

In planning your organizations fundraising program, you will have the information needed to demonstrate sustainability in a grant proposal. It is always easier to seek outside advice regarding the best ways to raise funds and then to compile the results and pull from the most promising suggestions. Seeking outside advice from successful business people and leaders can also help to expose your organization's mission and accomplishments to others who may be able and willing to help raise funds. Be prepared with tangible suggestions for innovative ways that businesses, etc. may contribute. For example: Matching dollars from business partners can be leveraged to draw down additional grant funds; While City, state, and/or private dollars finance the program's annual budget, Corporate sponsors pay for monthly field trips, etc.

Assessing organization's Sustain-ability is crucial in helping it to continue. When a sound fundraising program is in place, it is easier to adjust in the event that funding sources are cut or discontinued. Collaborative fundraising projects can help maximize resources to receive the best return on promotional investments.

Remember to consider the following when planning your fundraising program:

What type of funds or grants will be best for your organization? (Project grants, seed money, etc.)

It is important to thoughtfully consider your response to the following:

1. Who will lead your organizations fundraising campaign?

2. How will you maintain records of contacts and communication with potential funders?

3. How will you plan and document the results of meetings with potential funders?

4. How will you follow up on meetings with potential funders?

5. Who will research and categorize potential donors? (according to type of giving, application deadlines, contact information, etc.)

6. How can you assemble a Board or Committee especially to help with fundraising?

7. How will you generate quality grant proposals for your organization?

8. How will you determine your target donor market?

9. How will you convince donors that your organization is the ideal vehicle for their generosity?

DISCUSSION

Discuss some ideas or ways that your organization could generate funds.

_____
_____
_____
_____
_____
_____
_____
_____

Develop a simple work plan to carry out 3 of the ideas listed above.

Fundraising Activity	Duties Needed to Complete Activity

SUMMARY

The R.A.T.E.S. Principles concept was produced in response to the need for providing a consistent standard of development, practice and learning for non-profits and human service providers. It also proved to serve as a method to connect grassroots organizations, faith community leaders, government agencies and other stakeholders in order to join their resources.

For example, a group of service providers (for-profit companies, government agencies, grassroots organizations and clergy leaders) who attended a number of R.A.T.E.S. workshops decided to join forces to address substance abuse among ex-offenders. By the time a Request for Proposal was announced by the Department of Alcohol and Substance Abuse for a new initiative called *Access to Recovery*, several of the participants had already determined the foundation of their non-profits according to the R.A.T.E.S. Principles. They were able to use the results of the R.A.T.E.S. exercises as a method for assessing and demonstrating their readiness to participate in this new program. This group who had never worked together in such a capacity were ultimately celebrated as a notable example of an effective community based collaboration.

The leadership spearheaded by Rev. Dr. Aaron Jamal was able to teach R.A.T.E.S. Principles to a number of their clients who were then able to join them as service providers. It was so effective that the R.A.T.E.S. Principles were added to the program model so that *all* of the clients were exposed to it. This resulted in indoctrinating many of the clients into taking an active role in their own recovery. This team of service providers had one of the more successful Peer-led programs recorded by the *Access to Recovery* program. Unfortunately, the significant lack of attention to *Sustain-ability* as well as gaps in applying the *Response-ability* principle hindered their efforts from continuing. However significant lessons were realized and the effectiveness of applying R.A.T.E.S. Principles was demonstrated as well as documented.

The R.A.T.E.S. Principles offer a universal standard communication and operations to help build non-profit and human service strategies for successful program delivery. They also assist with building effective tools to allow non-profit leadership, organizations and agencies to work together *with* their clients to truly impact and change lives and communities.

Other Titles by Dr. Margaret Jamal

Faith Legacies- Guide for Faith-Based Nonprofits

My Grant Writing Secrets

National Treasures- Foundation Grants

When Girls Don't Tell

INDEX

www.ingramcontent.com/pod-product-compliance
Lightning Source LLC
Chambersburg PA
CBHW081354280526
45788CB00009B/2873